FOR THE LOVE OF GOD

CHELSEA PERRY

Published by Citadel Publishing
P.O. Box 846
Chesterfield, MO 63006
CitadelPublishing.org
publishing@chelseaperry.com

Photo credit by Ashley Becker
Cover design by Kuntara
Cover art by Chelsea Perry
Cover design contributors: Dan Chancellor and Libby Littrell
Circle of Relationships Visual by Will Weidler

ISBN: 979-8-9877348-0-3

Printed in the United States of America

TABLE OF CONTENTS

FOREWORD

The book before you is designed to stir your faith, strengthen your confidence, and give you a go-to resource to help you practically navigate your life.

My daughter Chelsea is a deeply committed person—committed to God, to her own personal destiny, and to lifting others.

This book she's worked so diligently to produce will fuel your devotion. By that, I mean this: using this book daily will help you develop a consistent rhythm with God and His Word which will fortify and strengthen you.

—PASTOR JEFF PERRY

HOW TO UTILIZE THIS BOOK

This book is only as powerful as the lasting impact that comes from reading it, retaining it, and applying it to your life. Because of this, I have organized each section into three parts for you to reference easily.

The first section is my perspective on each specific topic. I have over 20 years of pastoral experience and have mentored thousands of young and mature people from different countries and cultures to overcome the themes I address in this book. This book gives everyone access to the one-on-one guidance I've been able to share that's transformed entrepreneurs, parents, students, office workers, and countless others from all walks of life worldwide.

The second section is a personalized prayer that I crafted for you to pray over yourself to help bring peace and actively overcome whatever you face each day. Whether you realize it or not, verbalized prayers change situations, and I know these prayers will be just what you need in your time of need.

Finally, I have spent hours providing personalized scripture declarations inspired by the Bible that I rewrote in my own words in the first person so that you can speak over yourself to help combat life's difficult circumstances.

FOR THE LOVE OF GOD

This book is not designed for a closet or shelf; instead, I recommend keeping it in your purse, backpack, or briefcase to make it easily accessible throughout the day. It's meant to be kept near your coffee maker or bedside so you can quickly access it when you need it most. This reference guide for your life is not meant just to be read once chronologically but read and referenced over and over again when you find yourself facing off with the different themes of this book. Thankfully, you won't always deal with or relate to some of these topics, but when you do, these truths will be right there to hold your hand and walk you through.

If you're anything like me, you can cover it with stickers, underline it, and highlight it. You can buy a bunch of copies and decorate them to pass out to your friends. If you're like some of my friends, you might want to read with a ruler and make perfect lines under the parts that touch you most. The cool thing is there are no rules. Regardless of how you choose to read and reference this, I know it will change your life.

I want to hear how this book impacts your life! Connect with me and tell me! Find me online, and let me know how this changed your world when you read it!

Chapter 1

ANXIETY

To me, a big component of anxiety is the fruit of *worrying*. It comes from anticipating the worst; it's a buildup of stress! It's from not taking care of ourselves, and it can *creeeeep* up even on the most well-meaning, high-functioning individuals.

Instead of living with a constant hum of stress, a lot of us, including me, are learning to face off with it when it rears its ugly head. This mental anguish impacts the rich, the poor, the old, the young, and everyone in between. Feeling overwhelmed by life can come in waves, but God calms the storms of life. Where does this stress come from? I think two of the major areas are:

The pressure to succeed. The distance between expectation and reality, who we are, and the person we think we should be causes the tension of mental unrest (and makes you feel like you're going through the washing machine).

The lack of healthy relationships. The more time we spend on technology and the less time we spend interacting with humans leads to a rise in worry. Then, when we finally are together in person, it feels awkward, like we are strange and needy.

So we need tools to deal with this epidemic. Here is a checklist I do when I need to navigate through anxiety that you can use:

1. **Tell someone you trust.**

   I out myself to a friend. Bringing the feelings from the dark into the light almost instantly changes the panicked, heart-racing, alone feeling to a more manageable place.

2. **Check to see if your basic human needs are being met.**

   Someone once told me that I should treat myself like a baby. Weird, right? It sounds strange out of context, but I have seen what I become when I am not taking care of myself. I'm worn down, something weird happens, and then my body goes into fight-or-flight mode. If I haven't been taking care of myself, I can't respond in a healthy way to situations in life.

   Let's look at our basic needs:

   - Water—Shockingly, it's easy not to drink water. So do whatever it takes to drink water. Get a new water jug or water bottle. This is one of the basic but crucial essentials in life. Simple but not easy.
   - Food—Eat from the earth, eat the rainbow (a variety of different colors of fruits and veggies), and eat food your body can recognize.
   - Exercise—This could change seasonally! Do what you have to do to stay inspired by switching up your exercise. You only get one body, so stay strong and flexible and love the body you're in. If you get out of your routine, that's okay; get back in or start a new one! Do what works, ideally something you enjoy!
   - Sleep—We need sleep. Our bodies recharge and reset while we sleep! So, figure this area

out! I understand if this isn't a natural thing for you like it isn't for me, but I am finally convinced that we can't give what we don't have, and we get some of that by sleeping!

So treat yourself like a baby! If you feel full of anxiety, check to see if you are meeting your basic human needs.

3. **Work to resolve conflict.**

"If it is possible, as far as it depends on you, live at peace with everyone" (Romans 12:18). This scripture has served me well. What do I do when I am tormented but want to sleep? I figure out how I can bring peace to this situation if I even can. Is this out of my control? Is the other person ready to talk about it? Am I seemingly frustrated about a problem with a waitress in front of me at a restaurant when, in reality, that's *not* what I am mad about? Instead, my mind is racing to take out what I am *really* upset about on everything else.

I'm reminded of the scripture about the plank in our eye and the splinter in someone else's. I have to get my heart right first; then I can see if I need to talk to someone to get into the clean-heart club. That isn't a real club unless we start it. Also, I have dealt a lot with worrying about the past. Am I alone in this? I love that I evaluate my behavior. I do that on purpose, and it yields good fruit, but going into a cycle of too much ruminating over the past can lead to self-sabotage. I have learned that worrying about the past, present, or future doesn't do any good. Let me repeat this. Worrying in any form does not yield any fruit other than anxiety, stomachache, and maybe isolation.

To resolve the conflict, forgive other people and keep your own heart right with God, which only you are responsible for. You can always tell Him anything; He always forgives us and wants to make things right. The rest of the factors are things we often can't control!

4. **Don't procrastinate.**

Get your work done if you can. Don't put off until tomorrow what you can get done today. If you have to do something, face off with it instead of having a simple task drag on for several days, adding to the dread and making that thing much more significant than it is. For example, when going to an event, I'll get completely ready early and then rest. I find that the dread feels like there is a spider in the room, and when I don't procrastinate, it's amazing how much deeper my breaths are and how much more peaceful I am. Sometimes I just say, "Do it, Chelsea! Go, go, go," and cheer myself on. You have to be your own cheerleader!

5. **Have *fun!***

What brings you joy? I was talking to a group of friends about what puts a smile on my face, and it was wild what was on this list. I am naturally on the sunny side of life, but I also work to stay that way. I work on my coping skills; I resolve conflict quickly, write in a journal, talk to friends, keep my relationships healthy, work to grow emotionally, etc. But when it comes to finding things that simply bring me joy, they are hard to find. I am on a quest to find more things! More adventures! More fun! More dance parties!

Joy is a beautiful currency in life and should be free-flowing every day! We must be living a life that is full of *joy*. So where can I find this joy? I try to remember to bust out dancing every day. This is a good example for your friends, family, and kids. That freedom, fun, and laughter are even good for your health and healing to your peace, physical heart, and energy. It's saying, *I trust You to carry this, God. I don't have to take it all myself. I trust You so much that I will have fun while I do the dishes and while I spray down the counter, and while I drive and do everything in between.*

Who says you have to be sad? Who says you have to be drudging through life? Joy is contagious. Joy is a habit. Bound out of bed. Bop around the house. Get your favorite bubble bath, flowers, candles, blankets, cologne—surround your life, *all* five senses, with joy producers. Live an intentional life! Whatever brings you joy, surround yourself with it as often as possible! You can't give what you don't have, so fill up that joy tank!

Refuse a limited life! No more negative thinking or scrutinizing self-talk. We have all been too hard on ourselves. It's an honor to be alive. Let's ask God what we are here for and obey Him. This is our one big, beautiful life made up of a string of days. Those days are primarily full of everyday tasks. Can we make life's ordinary simplicity something to celebrate? Who else will if you don't?!

> I've got joy
> In the morning
>
> I've got joy
> At noon
>
> I've got joy
> In the evening
> How about you?
>
> Joy, joy, joy!

Anything or anyone coming to steal my joy cannot take it. So why not fight for it? The joy of the Lord is my *strength*. So why not be a joy-filled person? Fill your life with more things that provide joy! Even and especially the little things!

6. **Surround yourself with people who challenge you spiritually.**

   "As iron sharpens iron, so one person sharpens another" (Proverbs 27:17). A huge theme in this book is keeping yourself filled up spiritually. When you hang out with other people who are on the same page as you, it helps to keep you motivated in the same direction in any area, good or bad. This is why we must keep close to our hearts those we want to influence our decisions and impact our choices. They are usually destination determiners. It doesn't mean we can't be acquaintances and even friends with different people; it just means we have to be wise about those with whom we keep a close, steady pace on our life's marathon.

7. **Wait on God; His timing is perfect.**

   Do what you've got to do to bring God's peace on you. Fight to enter into God's rest and trust in His timing, and then remind yourself of it 50 million times. Easier said than done, but it is accurate and true that He can be trusted. I always remember that as much as I care about something, He cares about it more, and *I agree with Him!*

   I thought it was bizarre when I first heard the scripture that says to "make every effort" to enter into God's rest (Hebrews 4:11). Why would I have to work to enter into something so peaceful? But as I have thought about it, it makes sense. What else in my life is fought against more than my rest? I have to fight *hard* to enter into rest.

8. **Remember that your satisfaction is in God.**

   He is your fulfillment and your all-in-all. That's where your identity comes from. You are not satisfied in what you do or in a person but in God.

9. **Fear no one and nothing but God.**

   Remind yourself of the last two points (#7 and #8) a million more times a day as well.

10. **Speak God's Word.**

    When I am *majorly* in a battle, I put scriptures from the Bible about whatever I am facing all over my life. I put them in my car, in the kitchen, in my office, on the phone—*everywhere!* This is to combat the bombardment of fear. We need to counteract fear by building our faith.

    Faith comes by hearing the Word of God. When I was dealing with a substantial mental battle of fear, I had to override it with an onslaught of faith by *flooding* my heart with who God is and what He is capable of. I *stopped* allowing myself to look at what was producing fear and instead looked at the things that would build my faith. This has gotten me out of the dungeon of anxiety, fear, and torment.

SCRIPTURES USED IN THIS SECTION

"Then they cried out to the Lord in their trouble, and he brought them out of their distress. He stilled the storm to a whisper; the waves of the sea were hushed. They were glad when it grew calm, and he guided them to their desired haven."

—PSALM 107:28-30

"How can you say to your brother, 'Brother, let me take the speck out of your eye,' when you yourself fail to see the plank in your own eye? You hypocrite, first take the plank out of your eye, and then you will see clearly to remove the speck from your brother's eye."

—LUKE 6:42

"Who of you by worrying can add a single hour to your life? Since you cannot do this very little thing, why do you worry about the rest?"

—LUKE 12:25-26

"Do not grieve, for the joy of the LORD is your strength."

—NEHEMIAH 8:10B

"As iron sharpens iron, so one person sharpens another."

—PROVERBS 27:17

"Let us, therefore, make every effort to enter that rest, so that no one will perish by following their example of disobedience."

—HEBREWS 4:11

"Consequently, faith comes from hearing the message, and the message is heard through the word about Christ."

—ROMANS 10:17

ANXIETY

A PRAYER AGAINST ANXIETY

Okay, God, I'm looking to You
Do what only You can do
I give You my heart of devotion
Even if what surrounds me is a bunch of commotion
Anxiety, you have no hold on me
You no longer paralyze me
When you're not around, I'm a lion; I run this place
And when fear shows up, I ask for even more grace
So I say, get your grip unwrapped from my neck, fear
I'm not engaging with you, and you're not welcome here
You are no longer tricking me with your lies
I'm not going to be fooled, no longer mesmerized
The belief that my situation is out of control
Can't terrify me, no, not anymore
I give it to God; I invite You in
God, I know that this is where real peace begins
Do Your work here, my God
Do Your work here, my King
I need Your intervention in my suffering
Anxiety, *stop*! I'm done engaging with you!
I don't want to listen to what you're threatening to do
I take a deep breath in of reassurance and knowing
And I trust that even in this, I am growing
Thank You, God, I am steady and my feet are sure
And on You everything in my life is secure
I don't have to freak out or look to the left or the right
Or fear the pestilence that stalks in the night
I'm looking to You in every situation
And I won't worry no matter what goes on in my nation

SCRIPTURES USED IN THIS PRAYER

"Let your eyes look straight ahead; fix your gaze directly before you. Give careful thought to the paths for your feet and be steadfast in all your ways. Do not turn to the right or the left; keep your foot from evil." **—PROVERBS 4:25-27**

"You will not fear the terror of night, nor the arrow that flies by day, nor the pestilence that stalks in the darkness, nor the plague that destroys at midday." **—PSALM 91: 5-6**

PERSONALIZED SCRIPTURE DECLARATIONS TO COMBAT ANXIETY

PHILIPPIANS 4:6-7

I refuse to be anxious about anything, but instead, in every situation, I choose to pray, and I thank You, God, ahead of time, and I present my requests to You! Your peace is bigger than what I understand; it guards and protects my heart and my mind through You, Jesus.

1 PETER 5:6-7

I humble myself under Your mighty hand, God. I have no doubt You will lift me up at the right time and I am thankful for Your favor. I give You all of the things I am worried and stressed about because You care about me.

MATTHEW 6:25-27

God, You have told me not to worry about my life. Honestly, sometimes that is easier said than done, but I am working on this! I don't want to worry about where my next meal will come from or about my body; I don't want to be concerned with what I will wear. I know life is more than what I eat and my body more than what clothes I put on it. You told me to look at the birds; they do not plant seeds or reap a harvest or save food for later. But You feed them anyway! I know You care about them, and they are *birds!* You are the one who told us to consider them. You said, "Are people not much more valuable than birds! Can any of you, by worrying, add a single hour to your lives?" So I refuse to worry.

MATTHEW 6:31-34

I choose to stop worrying, trying to figure out what I'm

going to eat or what I'm going to wear. The people who don't believe in You, God, run after all these meaningless things, but you *know* that I need them. I look to You and seek Your kingdom first and what matters most to You, and I seek after Your righteousness because my desire is to be in right standing with You. I know from there everything else will be added to me! I refuse to worry about the future! Why would I? I have what I need for today! Tomorrow I will have what I need for then! Today I don't have what I need for tomorrow, so there is no need to tap into tomorrow's supply today by worrying! Tomorrow I will have enough to process, but I know I will have what I need when I get there!

PSALM 94:18-19

God, I am so thankful that every time I have been in a dark room of despair, Your unfailing love has supported me; You met me there and pulled me out. You have never left me. No matter how alone I have felt, You always have been there, even in the darkest night. When anxiety is a loud presence, I have been able to count on Your constant mercy. Even when everyone else seems to leave me, You are always near. Even if I can't feel Your presence, I know You're right beside me. Great is Your faithfulness!

JOSHUA 1:9

God, You have commanded me to only be strong and *very* courageous. So here I am, staying with You! No matter what! I say yes! I will be *bold,* and I will not be afraid. I *refuse* to be discouraged. *You* are my God and will be with me wherever I go, even when I can't feel it.

JOHN 14:27

Peace you leave with me; Your peace You provide for me. You give me peace in a unique way, unlike anybody else.

It's a supernatural, different kind of peace. There is *no way* I will let my heart be upset! I *refuse* to fear anything, but I *do* revere and respect You, God, and I care about what You think more than anything or anyone else!

2 TIMOTHY 1:7

Your Spirit, God, does not make me shrink back in a weak position but fills me with power, love, and self-discipline, which empowers me to accomplish Your will for my life! I do my work with all my heart like I am doing it for You. This is what helps me so much!

PROVERBS 12:25

Anxiety can weigh down my heart, but a kind word makes me happy and brings life to me.

ECCLESIASTES 11:10

God, I get rid of this anxiety from my heart, and I refuse to engage with it anymore! I get all of my troubles out of my body. I am not allowing them to dictate my decisions or my days.

1 JOHN 4:18

I know there is no fear in love. But perfect love drives out fear because fear has to do with punishment. The one who worries is not made perfect in love. So, God, I refuse to fear; please help me with this!

ISAIAH 41:10

So, God, I refuse to fear. You are with me, so I am con-fident that I will not be dismayed because You are my God. You will strengthen me and help me; You will hold me up with Your righteous right hand.

PSALM 56:3-4

When I am afraid, I put my trust in You, God, whose name I praise—in You alone I place my trust; then I am not afraid. What can mere mortals do to me?

PSALM 23:4

Even though I walk through the valley of the darkest night, I will fear no evil because You are with me; Your rod and Your staff comfort me.

PSALM 139:23-24

Search me, God, and know me inside and out; test me and know my deepest thoughts, the dreaming thoughts, and the anxious ones. See if there is any offensive way in me and lead me in a way that lasts forever.

LUKE 12:11-12

When I have important meetings and times with people I care about the most and intense days, I will not worry about what I will say because I know I will have the right words at the right time from the Holy Spirit.

PSALM 34:4

I looked for You, God, and You rescued me and saved me from all of my fears over and over again, and I am so thankful for it.

HEBREWS 13:6

Okay, so boldly, I say, "The Lord is my helper; I will not be afraid. What can people do to me?"

ISAIAH 35:3-4

God, I'm having a hard time today; please give me the strength I need for what I am facing. You know all things. Stabilize me. Make me steady for the tasks You have for me. Even though I am tired, strengthen my knees that try to buckle from underneath me; I say to the people around me who are dealing with fearful hearts, "Be strong! Do not be afraid; our God will come; He will be here with vengeance; He always has our backs! He will show up with divine retribution. He will get here to save us!" We can count on Him!

1 PETER 3:14

But even if I am under major attack and persecution for what is right, I am blessed. I do not fear their threats; I am not afraid.

ISAIAH 40:30-31

I put my hope in You, Lord; You renew and recharge my strength. I speak life over myself and say, "I soar on wings like eagles; I sprint and do not get tired; I walk, and I am not going to pass out."

JOHN 14:1

Because I believe in You, God, I refuse to let my heart be troubled.

ROMANS 8:37-39

In all things, I am more than a conqueror! I said more than a conqueror through You because You love me. The more I go on in my relationship with You, God, the more I am convinced that nothing can separate me from Your love. Death, life, angels, demons, the present, the future, no power or world ruler, there is nothing too high or low, there is nothing else in all creation that can separate me from You. Nothing. Nothing can separate us from Your love, God. Nothing.

PROVERBS 3:5-6

I trust in You, Lord, with all my heart, and I refuse to lean on what I know and understand; in all of the things that I do, I look to You, and You straighten every part of my crooked path.

JEREMIAH 17:7-8

How blessed is the one who trusts in You, Lord! So I throw every bit of my confidence over to You! I am like a tree planted by streams of living water that sends out its roots by the stream. I do not fear when the heat comes; my leaves are always green! I have no worries, even in a year of drought, and I never fail to bear good fruit.

COLOSSIANS 3:15

God, I let Your peace rule in my heart.

PSALM 55:22

I throw my anxieties on You, Lord, and You sustain me. You will never let the righteous be shaken. I'm so relieved You can be trusted; I can just lean back on this promise.

Chapter 2

BREAKTHROUGH

I lay in my dark bedroom and told the devil I would make him regret for the rest of my life the day he ever decided to mess with me! My body was covered with sores and swollen, and no one could tell me why. I told God I would take as many people with me to freedom as possible when I got out of my literal bed of hot fear and torment.

So here I am. Here is my breakthrough story. I am taking as many of you with me who want to come—to breakthrough, to freedom, and to a life of intentionality.

I started noticing my body was itching. I ignored it. Then it couldn't be ignored. I went to the dermatologist. The doctor didn't help. I don't even remember what she said. Then it started getting worse. I was just annoyed with my body. I was used to having a 20 out of 10 energy level. Before all this, I could push to make things happen, and my body always cooperated. I had never been in tune with my body up until this point. I was always a combination of impressed by and skeptical of the people who knew precisely how their body was responding from an almond or a tomato. I never could relate.

So there I was, disregarding the increasingly louder and louder alarming symptoms and pretending like none of them

B

were happening until it reached a point they could no longer be ignored. My life was about to change dramatically. I was about to go on an adventure that would lead to some of the answers I had been asking for, which led me to come closer to the version of a person I had been longing to become. This ordeal stripped layers off of me I didn't know I was hiding behind. I had *no idea* that breakthrough was on the other side of this lip swelling, body itching, and puffiness.

Five days after I went to the dermatologist (yes, I think she told me to bathe in oatmeal and use certain creams, something that didn't *scraatccchhh* the surface), I went to my first round of urgent care. The doctor gave me a steroid shot in my rear, told me I had urticaria (hives), and said, "I hate to tell you this, but some unfortunate schmucks get this, and it doesn't stop for upwards of a year."

Huh? I thought. *Well, that won't be me!*

(This was the beginning of my two-year ride with chronic urticaria, and I still get the little suckers on occasion! I had no idea what was ahead of me starting that day, but I am so glad I went through this experience because in going through it, my truer self was revealed. Layers came off and I became my more authentic self.)

He put me on prednisone (a steroid pack to calm the symptoms).

The hives were a little more tolerable while I was on the medicine. But then they came roaring back with a vengeance, and my lip looked like I had had bad plastic surgery.

I ignored it.

It subsided.

I do know this is a highly unhealthy plan. Feel free to skip ahead to the letter "J" if needed.

A few days later, I had just wrapped up a large and intense event, but I believe the issue wasn't just one busy event but more the exhaustion of doing too many things over a long time. At this time of my life, I wasn't asking God what was on His heart for me to do, even though I considered everything I

BREAKTHROUGH

was doing to be activities for Him. I kept living in this state of busyness for God, and it wasn't *about* Him; it was for Him.

But this is the scariest part; are you ready? I had no idea. With all my heart, I felt like my life was what I was supposed to be doing. I was mentoring, serving, pastoring, and still bearing great fruit. I am so proud of the musicals, songs, events, strategy, and the incredible people I contributed to during all that time. *However*, I am not sure what part God was originating and what part He was causing to work for my good.

For the record, I thought I was in perfect sync with God. But I wasn't. My body disengaged with me. It was giving me signals, and I wasn't listening to or even acknowledging them.

Eventually, I ended up in urgent care again, where they said that since my throat was closing, I had to go to the emergency room by ambulance because they feared I was going into anaphylactic shock.

Two gorgeous guys came in to take me to the ambulance. I mean, it seemed like it was fake. It was hilarious. I was lying there as a single girl looking like a duck, my throat was closing and I was all puffy, and these guys ended up being the world's most handsome paramedics I had ever seen. You've got to be kidding me. What are the odds? Of *course* they were. This was hilarious. I should've factored in the possibility of husband-potential responders. I was trying to make them laugh at least. I told my parents I was going to the hospital, and they met me there. So did one of my friends.

FROM THE BED TO THE FIRE

This led to a three-year process where I had to choose to fight to be well. I had to be my own advocate for my health.

Someone close to me said that many people build an identity around an illness. I had a choice to make. I could either stay in that place or walk out of that room. I chose at that moment to do whatever it would take to choose life and to step out of that room. I am forever thankful for that advice. I could've easily still been coddling this sickness if they hadn't told me that.

Also, that same person told me that I was in charge of my health care. This one is now very obvious to me after going through this process. No one cares about me like me—but wow, after watching doctors using search engines on the internet to look up my symptoms in front of me over and over again, my confidence started to wane. That's okay; that is why they call it practicing medicine.

God ended up using a whole team of people to get me well: a nutritionist, an allergist, a naturopath, nurses, and a chiropractor, but I know it was Jesus who led me through this process of healing. My lifestyle had to change. I had to change.

Later that year, I realized I could either be miserable in my bed or miserable on adventures, so I decided to go with my family to Nigeria and Israel. I am so glad I went! I went covered in hives and swollen. My brothers took horrible pictures of me that are also hilarious.

Africa changed my life. It was where I promised God that I would do whatever He asked. Again. On Reinhard Bonnke's stage, I committed myself back to God. I was all in. I would go wherever He told me to go and do whatever He told me to do. I saw people walking for miles to get to the meetings, carrying their babies and seats. It's a different kind of commitment to attend a service there than I have ever seen in the States. I heard some of them had been walking for days. They worshiped from a place inside so deep and undisturbed. It made an impression on me that can never be removed. There it was. Raw devotion. In the middle of a field. In the middle of the hottest heat. They wore the most colorful outfits and danced with total freedom, like their bodies kept the worship going.

It was so awakening to me as a pastor's daughter. Deep in my bones. Deep in my core. I was puffy and swollen and itchy. I didn't care. It was a life-defining moment for me. I picked up a rock from the gravel of that outdoor event. It was Bonnke's last. I have often said that rock is the most valuable thing I own.

DEFINING TURNING POINTS

A few months later, I went to Israel for my parents' fortieth wedding anniversary. Having all of their kids with them to renew their vows was a dream come true for them. I wasn't going to miss it. None of them knew how sick I was.

The good thing is, I'm happy most of the time, so people who weren't close to me couldn't tell I was suffering; they just knew I was heavier. That was from high doses of medicine. Most people didn't know what was going on with my health. I wasn't entirely alone; God sent people in to fight with me. God sent people to help me. But it was wild. You quickly discover what you are made of when you are in crisis.

I had to find my way forward every day, which meant taking the steps I knew to take daily. I would do whatever I could to see forward progress that day that I knew would lead me to momentum. So, daily steps of progress. My tasks were small increments of advancement to get me from here to there. Finding a way forward became my daily battle and goal. I refused to lose heart, lose hope, or lose sight of God and the other people attached to me. Keeping myself focused helped me to remember why I was in this fight. I was doing all I could and sometimes just *crawling* out of despair.

Some days I was working just to get out of bed.

Eventually, I was setting my shoes by the door and walking five minutes away from the house and five minutes back.

Then I was adding more time and becoming a consistent exerciser again. (Even though I missed my over-the-top adrenaline-inducing workouts, they were also hive-inducing). I got to start lifting weights again. I had actually missed that.

I tried all the things the dermatologist and other doctors recommended, and nothing was hitting the root cause. I am not here to give medical advice by any means. I'm just telling my story. I had a much more traditional approach to health care until I went through all this. Now I believe in a preventative lifestyle, but please still take me to the emergency room if needed.

God surrounded me with a team to fight my battle with me. Between emergency room visits, specialists, and different kinds of experts—I visited 27 doctors—and I tried to find the root cause. He brought me to a gifted naturopath (who is still a huge part of my healing process), who cleared me of metals and worked on my gut health, ran lots of tests, got me healthy enough, and taught me enough that I was prepared for my nutritionist.

She was sitting a few rows away from me at church. She saw me having to sit on a stool while speaking at church and, in her heart, knew she was supposed to help me. Eventually, we came together, and she transformed my entire approach to food. I started it all on a trip to Disney World. If you can do it there, you can do it anywhere.

She introduced me to a new way to eat and to the chiropractor. She wouldn't tell me about the chiropractor's unique approach; she just told me to go. Good thing because it was a little out of my comfort zone at the time. Now I can't even wait to get to her. I could hardly move, I was so sick, but I left better. Better and better every time I went. Once my gut was healthier, my food was in order, and she was doing her neuropathology and muscle testing, I started feeling better and better. I learned that things come in steps.

I had to make an effort to focus on the positive in this entire process. One trick for me to stay on the sunny side was the day when I got an allergy shot each month; I'd always look forward to their coffee. Surprisingly, they had this great coffee at their office, and I would anticipate it. I'd even bring my big cup from home to fill! The doctor was shocked at how much I loved his coffee machine, but again I was hunting for good in this process. I was going there to get a very

FOR THE LOVE OF GOD

I trust You in isolation station because, God, You're always true
You're working at midnight; You're working early too
You're working through lunchtime and in the afternoon
I choose to be patient and to endure what is building in me in this process
Like sandpaper, life is smoothing out my rough edges as I give You VIP access
I want You to upgrade me; completely rearrange me
I agree with You, God; I want to be what You intend for me to be
So let's step it up into the next atmosphere
I know it's time to go from here to there
And I am with You; I'm all in!
I don't want to slowly be okay with a little hidden heart sin
I want to live on that next level
Come on, God, I am Your rebel
Fully sold out, only fearing You
Living to do precisely what You tell me to do
I know life is filled with stress
But I didn't sign up to just perform, or behave, or strategize success
I'm ready to do exploits! Here I am! Send me, God! I am in utter devotion
I agree with You, God; my heart is an explosion
What does the ticket cost to go to the next place
I don't want to stay here shoving low-grade lies in my face
Whatever You are involved in is what I want to do
Wherever You go, Lord, I will follow You
I say yes to Your plans, to Your ways, to Your adventures
To Your assignments, myself I choose to indenture
Breakthrough, break free, time to break like a chain
I am sick of walking a circle in self-inflicted pain

No more spinning in traps of my mind

You didn't put me here, so why waste my time?

I reach around the cage and open up the lock

I fly out of the spot where I got myself stuck

Today I choose breakthrough and I fly away

From misery, from pain, I take my freedom; this I claim!

I am so excited! I enthusiastically rejoice

Before I feel it, I make a joyful noise

Oh, yes, it's bubbling out of me; this is the turning point—this is the linchpin

I praise You, God, for my breakthrough. Even before I feel it, I begin

SCRIPTURES USED IN THIS PRAYER

"So David came to Baal-perazim and he defeated them there, and said, 'The Lord has broken through my enemies before me, like a breakthrough of water.' So he named that place Baal-perazim (master of breakthroughs)." —**2 SAMU-EL 5:20, AMP**

"After saying this, he spit on the ground, made some mud with the saliva and put it on the man's eyes." —**JOHN 9:6**

"Ah, Sovereign Lord, you have made the heavens and the earth by your great power and outstretched arm. Nothing is too hard for you." —**JEREMIAH 32:17**

"Praise be to the LORD God, the God of Israel, who alone does marvelous deeds." —**PSALM 72:18**

"The LORD himself goes before you and will be with you; he will never leave you nor forsake you. Do not be afraid; do not be discouraged." —**DEUTERONOMY 31:8**

"God is our refuge and strength, always ready to help in times of trouble." **—PSALM 46:1, NLT**

"Let the morning bring me word of your unfailing love, for I have put my trust in you. Show me the way I should go, for to you I entrust my life." **—PSALM 143:8**

"The LORD will fight for you; you need only to be still." **—EXODUS 14:14**

"O God, you are my God, earnestly I seek you." **—PSALM 63:1A**

"My mouth is filled with your praise, declaring your splendor all day long." **—PSALM 71:8**

"I keep asking that the God of our Lord Jesus Christ, the glorious Father, may give you the Spirit of wisdom and revelation, so that you may know him better." **—EPHESIANS 1:17**

"He who has received His testimony has set his seal to this, that God is true." **—JOHN 3:33, NASB1995**

"But let patience have its perfect work, that you may be perfect and complete, lacking nothing." **—JAMES 1:4, NKJV**

"Whoever conceals their sins does not prosper, but the one who confesses and renounces them finds mercy." **—PROVERBS 28:13**

"For I always do what pleases him." **—JOHN 8:29B**

"But the people who know their God shall be strong, and carry out great exploits." **—DANIEL 11:32B, NKJV**

"Then I heard the voice of the Lord saying, 'Whom shall I send? And who will go for us?' And I said, 'Here am I. Send me!'" **—ISAIAH 6:8**

"Shout for joy to the LORD, all the earth." **—PSALM 100:1**

PERSONALIZED SCRIPTURE DECLARATIONS TO BRING BREAKTHROUGH

1 CORINTHIANS 10:13

I know that it is not unusual for me to deal with temptation since every person who has ever walked the face of the earth has had to deal with different enticements. This is a relief to me! I am not alone. God, You are faithful; You will not let me be tempted beyond what I can handle. But when I am allured, You provide a way out so that I escape the trap! So I choose to *run*! I take the way out You have prepared for me, no matter how attractive the seduction is.

ISAIAH 54:17

No weapon formed against me will work, and I rebuke every word spoken against me, and I claim favor over me! I can do this because it is a benefit of being a servant of You, God; You are my vindicator.

1 JOHN 5:14-15

God, I come to You with confidence. I know that You hear me, and I have what I ask of You as I request it according to Your will.

JOHN 8:32

When I know the truth, the truth sets me free.

MATTHEW 7:7-11

When I ask You for something, God, I believe it will be given to me. I seek You out, so I know I will find You. I knock, and I am confident the door will be opened to me. I know everyone who asks receives; the one who seeks finds;

to the one who knocks, the door will be opened. Which of us, if our son or daughter asks for bread, will give him or her a stone? Or if they ask for a fish, will give them a snake? Since we are normal people and even we know how to give good gifts to our kids, how much more will You, our Father in heaven, who has the whole world in Your hands, give good gifts to those who ask You?!

EPHESIANS 6:12

What I am fighting with is not against people; it's not with what I am and know in the world around me. But it is in the spirit realm; the battle of my life is with the rulers, the authorities, the powers of this dark world, and the spiritual forces of evil in the heavenly realms. God, You have given me authority over these things!

JEREMIAH 29:13

God, I seek You with my whole heart; that is how I find You!

HEBREWS 4:16

I boldly approach Your amazing throne of grace with confidence so that I can receive mercy and find grace to help me in my time of need.

MATTHEW 11:28-30

I go to You, Jesus, when I am weary, upset, exhausted, bogged down, and You give me rest. I take Your yoke upon me and learn from You because You are gentle and humble in heart, and there I always find rest for my soul. Your yoke is easy, and Your burden is light. (I strongly suggest you study this concept more because learning more about the whole "yoke" concept really brought a lot of clarity to this scripture for me.)

BREAKTHROUGH

B

PSALM 107:4-9

I was hungry and thirsty, and my life slowly drifted away. Then I cried out to You, Lord, in my trouble, and You delivered me from my distress. You led me by a straightforward way to a place where I could settle. I give thanks to You, Lord, for Your unfailing love and Your wonderful deeds. You satisfy the thirsty and fill the hungry with good things!

PSALM 119:35

Direct me in the path of Your truth because there I find delight!

PSALM 42:11

Why, my soul, are you so sad? Why so upset and swirling within me? I put my hope in You, God my Father. I praise You because You are my Savior and my King!

PSALM 51:10-12

Create in me a pure heart, O God, and renew a faithful and consistent spirit within me. Do not ban me from Your presence or take Your Holy Spirit from me. Restore to me the joy of Your salvation and give me a willing spirit; I know that will sustain me.

PSALM 34:19

God, even the people who are in right standing with You have troubles because we are human, and we are not exempt from *having* problems, but *You* get us through them all!

ROMANS 8:37

No matter what I face in life, I annihilate the enemy and *win* in a huge way through the power that God supplies, and it overwhelms the devil.

PHILIPPIANS 1:6

I am confident that You, God, who started this good work in me, will follow through with it until it is complete!

HEBREWS 13:8

Jesus, You are the same yesterday, today, and forever! You have delivered me in the past, and You will deliver me again. On You I set my hope. You will continue to deliver me **(2 Corinthians 1:10)**!

Chapter 3
CLARITY

That dull fog that mysteriously seems to creep in periodically and permeate every part of life is hard to snap out of sometimes, but waking up from it is necessary! I feel excited to be fully alive, completely alert, and aware of the things around me. When I slip into those times when I need to navigate, I find myself praying for clarity and wisdom from God. He knows just what to do. Right now, I draw near to Him and trust Him to the utmost.

The Bible shows how important it is to inquire of the Lord as King David did. So what does that mean in my real life? Ask God everything! I've learned that He likes to be included in our daily lives. I say to God, "What do You want to talk to me about this morning? What should I pray about? Should I go for a walk? According to Your plans, what does this day look like because that is what I am going for! On earth, as it is in heaven (see Matthew 6:10)! I agree with You, God! The more I invite You in, the more clarity I get!"

I am embarrassed to say I have lived years of my life just having Him "bless" the plans I've created for myself without having Him be the actual author and finisher of them. What is on Your heart, God? I have gone in and out of seasons where I have done better at asking than others.

Nothing should be on the throne of your heart but God. Anything can be an idol if it exalts itself above your relationship with Him. Are you ready for this? Even your calling or assignments for Him? Even the things you *do* for God at church? Even when you are trying to be a good person and even when you are running around trying to do it all for Him from a deeply rooted *good place?* Matthew 6:33 says to seek first His kingdom, and all these things will be added for you as well. Our identity can be wrapped around these things that we do, and we might not even be aware of it. It's all so intertwined that we can't differentiate it.

It's easy to see that the prodigal son in the Bible had things to work on, but can you see what the prodigal's brother was dealing with? I for sure relate to him in a lot of ways (see Luke 15:11-32). Feeling righteous because of my "works" and efforts in serving when I am not even sure all of those things were things I was supposed to do. At the time I did them, I thought they were awesome and from a good place, but I was on autopilot and wasn't checking in with the one who matters most (God that is). I mean, we were talking, just not about what I was doing for Him. It's amazing how this can creep up in our relationships too. We start serving and doing things we think we should, and the other person is like, *I didn't even need that.*

Distraction is such a sneaky trick. Especially when we are distracted by things we think we are doing for God or the ones we love. *Whoa, whoa, whoa.*

Here it is: when you mess up, get up. When you get distracted, get your focus back by fixing your eyes on what you want to grow. When it's time to work, build brick by brick, but do not get distracted. *Jesus* is the center of it all. Not anyone or anything else. Yes, we can't give what we don't have. We have to take care of ourselves. Yes, we get to serve God through our churches. *But* it is all about what it is all about: *Jesus.*

If it isn't, here is some clarity: it's time for it to be again. He loves us even when we forget.

Some of the most intelligent people I know understand that to strip something down to its roots and be able to explain it to a five-year-old, you have to understand it in its entirety. Do you know Him? *Go to the Source.* Clarity is face-to-face with *God.*

There is nothing I can't say to God. Can we please start to go to God in a raw, natural way? Clarity is in the honesty of our relationship with Him. That is where God sits. It means our priorities, our love, and our eyes are on Him.

The truth is that all of us need Jesus. Not a social media version of Him. Not a candy-coated distant version of Him. But the real, authentic, on-the-floor, deep, raw, right-to-the-heart version of Him. The one who spit in the dirt. The one who sets the captives free. That is my God. The one who sat with the woman at the well. The one who accepted and healed the woman with the issue of blood. The one that the kids ran up to. The one I love.

SCRIPTURES USED IN THIS SECTION

"And David inquired of the LORD, 'Shall I pursue this raiding party? Will I overtake them?'"
—1 SAMUEL 30:8A

"Looking unto Jesus, the author and finisher of our faith, who for the joy that was set before Him endured the cross, despising the shame, and has sat down at the right hand of the throne of God."
—HEBREWS 12:2, NKJV

"After saying this, he spit on the ground, made some mud with the saliva, and put it on the man's eyes."
—JOHN 9:6

"The Spirit of the Lord is on me, because he has anointed me to proclaim good news to the poor. He has sent me to proclaim freedom for the prisoners and recovery of sight for the blind, to set the oppressed free, to proclaim the year of the Lord's favor."

—LUKE 4:18-19

"He said to her, 'Daughter, your faith has healed you. Go in peace and be freed from your suffering.'"

—MARK 5:34

'Then, leaving her water jar, the woman went back to the town and said to the people, 'Come, see a man who told me everything I ever did. Could this be the Messiah?'"

—JOHN 4:28-29

"Then people brought little children to Jesus for him to place his hands on them and pray for them. But the disciples rebuked them. Jesus said, 'Let the little children come to me, and do not hinder them, for the kingdom of heaven belongs to such as these.'"

—MATTHEW 19:13-14

A PRAYER ON CLARITY

Right now, I take a deep breath in and let a deep breath out
I feel myself calming down no matter what I'm upset about
I am filled with the knowledge of God's will and know exactly what to do
There is absolutely no reason that I should be freaking out because I look to You
There is no fear here—it is just faith
So, fear, listen here: I laugh in your face
I am not in confusion; I'm not in a fog
I am living by the grace of the living God
I move in faith and know just what to do
You messed with the wrong person
I don't negotiate with you
My God moves mountains at the bend of His hand
I know that I can trust Him and I am in His plan
I see by faith, not by alarming circumstances
When others are freaking out, that's when I start the dances
God's Word lights my way and is a lamp on my path
So that is where I go to get my roadmap
Clarity comes as I focus myself
Mind, will, and emotions—sit on the shelf!
Spirit, rise and be front and center
Because there's a clarifying zone I choose to enter

SCRIPTURES USED IN THIS PRAYER

"For this reason, since the day we heard about you, we have not stopped praying for you. We continually ask God to fill

you with the knowledge of his will through all the wisdom and understanding that the Spirit gives." —**COLOSSIANS 1:9**

"Overhearing what they said, Jesus told him, 'Don't be afraid; just believe.'" —**MARK 5:36**

"For God is not a God of disorder but of peace—as in all the congregations of the Lord's people." —**1 CORINTHIANS 14:33**

"But by the grace of God I am what I am, and His grace to me was not without effect. No, I worked harder than all of them—yet not I, but the grace of God that was with me." —**1 CORINTHIANS 15:10**

"For we live by faith, not by sight." —**2 CORINTHIANS 5:7**

"He moves mountains without their knowing it and over-turns them in His anger." —**JOB 9:5**

"'For I know the plans I have for you,' declares the LORD, 'plans to prosper you and not to harm you, plans to give you hope and a future.'" —**JEREMIAH 29:11**

"Let them praise his name with dancing and make music to him with timbrel and harp." —**PSALM 149:3**

"Your word is a lamp for my feet, a light on my path." —**PSALM 119:105**

things that I do not know right now and that I cannot figure out on my own!

PSALM 119:105

God, Your Word is a lamp for my feet and a bright light on my path.

Chapter 4

DEPRESSION

People seem so sad, and many doctors seem happy to write out prescriptions, and it feels like society is getting sicker by the minute. I also see the value in rebuilding the chemicals in your brain with medicine when you need to for a season while under a great doctor's supervision. I am by no means saying you shouldn't. I know there is a time and place for that; however, sadness and busyness and numbing out seem like a cycle that hasn't stopped for much.

Depression and worry, fear and regret—the whole circle of life seems to be messed up in the head. Depression is connected to our spirit, soul, and body, and it takes focusing on all of those areas to get freedom from it! In the times I have experienced it, I have learned that in the darkness, if I focus on a pinhole of light, no matter how small that light is, eventually, that pinhole becomes stars that fill my life's sky. Eventually, it will turn into the day if you make that central. It's amazing what perspective will do.

Like most people, I have had significant moments of darkness when it felt like God forgot my zip code. I remember feeling like things were so stuck in my life that I wasn't sure how to get back to myself, much less to "where I was

47

D

supposed to be." Whatever that means. This longing to be somewhere or someone or to *achieve* "something" can plague us. *But* I have learned to relinquish control of the outcome—so far, it's working. We do our part; God does the rest. But for years, I was feeling behind. Whose schedule are we on anyway? Does God cause all things to work together for those who love Him or not? Is He a good God or not?! Okay, He can be trusted!

But life is weird, people are weird, I am weird, circumstances are weird, and we must be committed to overcoming and never quit, no matter what. There are lives attached to us. I remember seeing a picture of myself as a little girl with bright red lipstick on and eyes full of happy joy and peace. I looked at my past self and thought I would never be her again. Then I decided to fight to get her back, but I wasn't sure how. I learned that we don't know what we need half the time. But I decided that any way I could find a way forward, I would take. I prayed for God to help me.

I remember my first round of circumstantial depression at age 25 after a myriad of events stacked against me one after the next. I wasn't in tune with myself, acknowledging how I felt, so I couldn't talk to people to get help. I was on staff at my parents' church, living at their house and crying myself to sleep every night. One night, my mom came and found me and asked me what was wrong. It was about to go down. I finally told her. I started unraveling the knots that were eating me up inside. With the feeling of utter isolation and literally crying to my mom on my bed, I felt pretty low. She asked why I didn't come to them and explain what was happening before then. I told her it just was so hard even to know what was happening, let alone explain it. My mom coming in to talk to me was a pinhole of light in my night, creating a star of hope in my sky of devastation.

Then my parents brought one of my best friends to town for my birthday. I had stopped taking care of myself. My face was broken out. I had lost my desire to get fixed up, and we were getting ready for church.

Looking at me, she said, "What are you wearing?"

"This," I said, referring to an outfit that looked as sad and lame as I felt.

"Where is my best friend?" she asked.

"This is the new me," I replied.

Experts say that if cats stop grooming themselves, watch them because something might be wrong. I think humans are the same way. If we don't take care of our bodies and stop grooming ourselves, it is an outward sign of what's going on inside our hearts. There are many ways humans express this: isolating themselves, becoming rude, comfort eating, or the more subtle one—becoming a workaholic and hiding in their activity. (That one is hard to detect! Don't ask me how I know.)

My friend knew the signs that I wasn't doing well, so she planned a shopping trip to the mall for us to get heels as a physical expression that she wasn't letting me give up on life. (Other people might love this, but shopping honestly isn't my thing. However, I knew it was a step forward in the right direction.)

Her arrival in my town was another pinhole of light in the darkness that had become my reality. That shopping trip was another pinhole. Little by little, I started celebrating those small victories until the pinholes of light took over the sky, and my darkness became day again.

I know God has that for you, but you are the only one who can fight for yourself. God will send help, but you must fight from within. Find a way forward. Start right now. Focus on a pinhole of light at a time. It has a cumulative effect. You will be shocked at how much ground you will take by just starting. Lives will be impacted around you if you begin to take care of yourself; you'll eventually build momentum in the *right* direction.

I have learned since then that when I notice that I have a sad cluster of feelings trying to creep up on me, I have to

D

communicate clearly to the close circle around me. Otherwise, it can sneak in and try to turn into a season instead of a moment. I get on top of it immediately and tell it where to go!

SCRIPTURES USED IN THIS SECTION

"And we know that in all things God works for the good of those who love him, who have been called according to his purpose."

—ROMANS 8:28

"For the Lord is good; his steadfast love endures forever, and his faithfulness to all generations."

—PSALM 100:5, ESV

DEPRESSION

A PRAYER ON DEPRESSION

You lying, disgraceful symptoms from hell

Get away from me today and break this evil spell

I do not agree or engage with you

You can stop right now; I'm telling you, we're through

If my chemicals are off, then I say get back in line

If I need to make changes, I'll do it; that's fine

I'll take a walk, call a friend, and refuse to quit

But as for the spiritual battle, I'll choose to resist

Mind, stop racing and wandering about!

I focus on things without confusion and doubt

There is no fear that I'll allow to consume me

Those feelings of upset that try to undo me

I say right now, just stop right there!

Be quiet, calm down, you are not welcome here!

Peace be still as I navigate my heart

I live the truth in every way; I want this fresh start

I've seen depression take down kingdoms and level marriages flat

Well, I refuse to let this happen here! My life won't be like that

I ask for healing in my heart so I can be what You've called me to be

I look to You, God; I know You are always at work in me

I know You complete the works You start; You finish what You author

You are the repairer of the breach; You are the ultimate heart doctor

So I can trust You, my King; I don't lean on what I understand

I choose to rely on You because I can trust in Your plan

I'd rather go with You and have your way for my life

It's so much better anyway, fulfilled and peaceful, without strife
There is no more suffering when I look to You
Your peace washes over me as You always see me through

SCRIPTURES USED IN THIS PRAYER

"Submit yourselves, then, to God. Resist the devil, and he will flee from you." —**JAMES 4:7**

"For our struggle is not against flesh and blood, but against the rulers, against the authorities, against the powers of this dark world and against the spiritual forces of evil in the heavenly realms." —**EPHESIANS 6:12**

"Finally, brothers and sisters, whatever is true, whatever is noble, whatever is right, whatever is pure, whatever is lovely, whatever is admirable—if anything is excellent or praiseworthy—think about such things." —**PHILIPPIANS 4:8**

"And he awoke and rebuked the wind and said to the sea, 'Peace! Be still!' and the wind ceased, and there was a great calm." —**MARK 4:39, ESV**

"And he who was seated on the throne said, 'Behold, I am making all things new.' Also he said, 'Write this down, for these words are trustworthy and true.'" —**REVELATION 21:5, ESV**

"Heal me, LORD, and I will be healed; save me and I will be saved, for you are the one I praise." —**JEREMIAH 17:14**

"Being confident of this, that he who began a good work in you will carry it on to completion until the day of Christ Jesus." —**PHILIPPIANS 1:6**

"Fixing our eyes on Jesus, the pioneer and perfecter of faith. For the joy set before him he endured the cross, scorning

its shame, and sat down at the right hand of the throne of God." **—HEBREWS 12:2**

"Those from among you shall build the old waste places; you shall raise up the foundations of many generations; and you shall be called the Repairer of the Breach, The Restorer of Streets to Dwell In." **—ISAIAH 58:12, NKJV**

"But I trust in you, LORD; I say, 'You are my God.'" **—PSALM 31:14**

"And the peace of God, which transcends all understanding, will guard your hearts and your minds in Christ Jesus." **—PHILIPPIANS 4:7**

D

DEPRESSION

PERSONALIZED SCRIPTURE DECLARATIONS TO FIGHT DEPRESSION

PSALM 9:9

God, Your presence is where I run to when I am at my worst and when I'm doing great. You are a castle wall when I am going through a hard time! Through highs and lows, You are consistent.

PSALM 30:5

Even though tonight I might cry all night long, tomorrow morning there will be triumphant happiness because when the sun comes up, I can smile and say to myself, welcome to your new mercies!

PSALM 30:11-12

You have turned my crying into a dance party! You have replaced my sad clothes that I wear when I am upset with joy, joy, joy, and You have filled my heart with a new song. I will give You thanks forever!

PSALM 34:17-18

Here I am, Lord; I cry out to You, and I know You hear me. You deliver me from all my troubles. You always have, and You always will. Lord, You are close to the broken-hearted, and You save those who are in despair.

PSALM 40:2-3

You lift me out of the darkest place, out of the hardest heart seasons that feel impossible to escape from, yet You are there! Fixing my eyes on You gets and keeps me out of the offense. You set my feet on Your steady foundation and give me a firm place to stand! You put a new song in my mouth, a hymn of praise to You, my God. Many will see and revere You, Lord, and put their trust in You. I know I do!

PSALM 143:7-9

I need a quick answer, Lord; I'm needing help! Do not hide Your face from me, or I will be like those who fall into trouble and go down to the pit! Let the morning bring me word of Your unfailing love because I have placed my trust in You. It's always been You! It will always be You! Show me the way I should go; to You I entrust my life. Rescue me from my enemies, Lord; I hide myself in You.

ISAIAH 40:31

I put my hope in You, Lord, and that is where my strength is renewed. Because of You, I can do things with ease, like the eagle takes to flight. I run and do not get exhausted.

JOHN 10:10

The thief comes to steal, to kill, and to destroy. Jesus, You came that I may have life and have it to the absolute fullest.

PHILIPPIANS 4:8

Whatever is authentic, upstanding, accurate, true to the core, graceful, excellent—if anything is exemplary or honorable—I process and meditate on those things. If it isn't all of these things, it doesn't fit my thinking criteria!

DEUTERONOMY 31:8

Lord, You go before me and stay with me and will never turn Your back on me. I will not be afraid; I refuse to be discouraged.

D

PSALM 32:10

God, Your unfailing love surrounds me. I put my trust in You.

2 CORINTHIANS 1:3-4

You are the one and only true God. The God of compassion and the God of all comfort. You console me when times get rough so that I can extend the same love I have only experienced by Your presence to the brokenhearted in any trouble with the same warmth I have received.

PSALM 37:23-24

You, oh Lord, make my steps sure when I delight in You, when I look to You, when I take notice of the things that matter most to You. When those things that are central to You are central to me, then my steps are sure. When my eyes veer off to lesser things, that's when I stumble. But when I look to You, You get me back on track; and because of You, I will not fall, even when I trip, because You uphold me with Your powerful hand!

NEHEMIAH 8:10

God, Your joy is my strength.

DEPRESSION

Chapter 5
EATING

I want to encourage you with this topic to ask God what He has for you with your food. I have had such an interesting time exploring this and discovering the best approach for different seasons of my life, how much energy I am putting out, and, therefore, how much I need. In this section, I am not presenting a theory but more laying out some information I have found for you to observe with me.

I'm constantly gathering research about what the Bible says about food to gain a comprehensive biblical perspective on eating. Let's dive in and look together at just *some* of what the Bible has to say about our body's life source: *food!*

It's intriguing to me how Jesus interacted with food in the Bible: the last supper, "breaking bread," communion to represent His blood and body, preparing "a table" in the presence of our enemies. Food facilitates so much meaningful interaction in the Bible. Jesus' first miracle was turning water into wine at His mom's request at a wedding (see John 2:1-11). Interesting. He multiplied the loaves and fish (see Matthew 14:13-21). He went to lunch with the tax collector, Zacchaeus, who was known to take more money than he was supposed to from the taxpayers! After his lunch with Jesus, he gave everyone back the money he took and *more* (see Luke 19:1-10). All of these things are fascinating to me. There is also talk of not judging people for what they feel led to eat or what not to eat and how God gave us food to enjoy.

Eating is something we do every day. We have to eat to fuel our bodies. It's also a place where we gather and prepare a table with our loved ones to facilitate memories and express our hearts. The devil tempted Jesus with food. That is pretty wild.

So, my takeaway on this is that food is a unique subject, and the Bible has a lot to say about it. It is very personal to each individual. I don't see broad rules or brushstrokes on this. Instead, I see a few key guidelines.

We don't judge other people for what they eat. We are free to eat what we feel the liberty to eat or not to eat. There is spiritual food we can rely on every day, and there are good specific references to that. But we are responsible to get it by seeking God, getting in the Bible, praying, worshiping, and drawing near to Him.

So, living a fasted lifestyle (moderation and restraint) submitted to God even in my eating is important. Keeping my entire life yielded to God is imperative to my walk with Him. But food is personal. It's only between God and us. It's none of my business what other people eat. It's okay for me to eat what I feel like I'm supposed to and for others to eat what they are supposed to, depending on what God is releasing them to eat for their bodies and seasons. Monitoring my food has helped me get healthy in different seasons, but it can quickly become an idol. What I have learned from my study of this is to not judge other people for what they eat, to ask God how He feels about what I'm eating, and to know that it's a matter of the heart. And when I prepare a meal for my family, it is from a place of love, and so many beautiful things happen around that table.

SCRIPTURES USED IN THIS SECTION

"After taking the cup, he gave thanks and said, 'Take this and divide it among you. For I tell you I will not drink again from the fruit of the vine until the kingdom of God comes.' And he took bread, gave thanks and broke it, and gave it to them, saying, 'This is my body given for you; do this in remembrance of me.' In the same way, after the supper he took the cup, saying, 'This cup is the new covenant in my blood, which is poured out for you.'"

—LUKE 22:17-20

"And they devoted themselves to the apostles' teaching and the fellowship, to the breaking of bread and the prayers."

—ACTS 2:42, ESV

"You prepare a table before me in the presence of my enemies. You anoint my head with oil; my cup over-flows."

—PSALM 23:5

"Those who feel free to eat anything must not look down on those who don't. And those who don't eat certain foods must not condemn those who do, for God has accepted them."

—ROMANS 14:3, NLT

"The devil said to him, 'If you are the Son of God, tell this stone to become bread.'"

—LUKE 4:3

"But not everyone possesses this knowledge. Some people are still so accustomed to idols that when they

E

EATING

*eat sacrificial food they think of it as having been sac-
rificed to a god, and since their conscience is weak, it
is defiled. But food does not bring us near to God; we
are no worse if we do not eat, and no better if we do."*

—1 CORINTHIANS 8:7-8

"Give us today our daily bread."

—MATTHEW 6:11

A PRAYER ON EATING

Eating is something I do every day

But, God, I'm with You; I want to do it Your way

I want everything I eat to glorify You

Let me know what You're thinking; show me what to do

I want to honor You with everything, even with what I put in my face

To eat to be healthy, not to fill up some space

I know food is to fuel my body and I want to be on course

This is an interesting topic and I want to be Your force

I want to be what You made me to be: strong every day

I don't want to be full of gas station snacks and so tired, no way

Help me to view food the way You want me to

So I can do the things You've called me to do

It's amazing how much Your Word has to say on this topic specifically

I am looking to You to give me direction; I want to be functioning magnificently

Day by day, I look to You

You know best what I should do

There is no room in my life that You cannot enter

From summer, spring, fall to winter

You have provided all I need. I look to You

I invite You in, even into my food

I don't lean on what I understand

You are the author and finisher, even over my eating plan

We choose our ways, but You direct our steps

So, God, help me out because You know my body best

This is Your temple; You dwell in me

I want to honor You, even in what I eat!

SCRIPTURES USED IN THIS PRAYER

"So whether you eat or drink or whatever you do, do it all for the glory of God." **—1 CORINTHIANS 10:31**

"Show me your ways, LORD, teach me your paths." **—PSALM 25:4**

"That each of them may eat and drink, and find satisfaction in all their toil—this is the gift of God." **—ECCLESIASTES 3:13**

"And my God will meet all your needs according to the riches of his glory in Christ Jesus." **—PHILIPPIANS 4:19**

"Trust in the LORD with all your heart and lean not on your own understanding." **—PROVERBS 3:5**

"And whatever you do, whether in word or deed, do it all in the name of the Lord Jesus, giving thanks to God the Father through him." **—COLOSSIANS 3:17**

E

EATING

PERSONALIZED SCRIPTURE DECLARATIONS ON WHAT GOD HAS TO SAY ABOUT FOOD

HOW SHOULD I EAT?

GENESIS 1:29

God, in the beginning, You gave us every seed-bearing plant on the face of the whole earth and every tree that has fruit with seeds in it! You said they are ours to eat.

GENESIS 9:3

God, You said that everything that lives and moves will be food for us. Just as You gave us the green plants, You now give us everything.

PROVERBS 27:7

God, I know that when I am full, I could even hate the sweet taste of honey, but when I am hungry, even what is bitter tastes sweet.

PSALM 136:25

You give food to every creature. Your love endures forever.

SPIRITUAL FOOD

MATTHEW 12:50

Whoever fulfills Your purpose and follows You, God, will be my brother, my sister, and my mother. *They* are my family.

DEUTERONOMY 8:3

I don't live on bread alone but on every word that comes from the mouth of God.

JOHN 6:27

Jesus, You told us that You do not work for food that goes rotten but for food that remains until eternal life. That is what You have placed Your seal of approval on, God.

PSALM 107:9

You satisfy the thirsty and fill the hungry with good things.

MATTHEW 5:6

Blessed are those who hunger and thirst for righteousness because we will be filled.

JOHN 4:34

My food is to do Your will, God. You are the one who sent me, and I am here to finish *Your* work. What's on *Your* heart is on *my* heart!

JOHN 6:35

Jesus, You declared that You are the bread of life. Whoever comes to You will never go hungry, and whoever believes in You will never thirst again.

MATTHEW 6:9-13

My Father who is in heaven, I worship Your name; Your kingdom come, Your will be done, on earth as it is in heaven. Give me today my daily bread and forgive me my debts, as I also have forgiven my debtors. You lead me not into temptation but deliver me from the evil one.

MATTHEW 6:25

You have told me not to worry about my life, what I will eat or drink, or about my body—what I will wear. Life is more than food, and the body more than clothes.

MATTHEW 4:4

Jesus, You said, "Man should not live on actual food alone," but instead You instructed us to live by every word that comes from Your mouth, God.

2 CORINTHIANS 9:10

God, You are the one who supplies seed to the sower, so I can give and sow into other people's lives. You give food for me to eat, and You also supply and increase my store of resources to invest. That way, I always have something for now, for later, and to invest into the lives around me that will enlarge my intentional impact investment.

FREEDOM IN FOOD

E

ROMANS 14:3

The one who eats everything with freedom should in no way be critical or loath the one who has no freedom in this area, and the one who does not eat everything with freedom should not judge the person that does because You, God, have accepted us all.

1 CORINTHIANS 8:8

Food does not bring us near to You, God; we are no worse if we do not eat something and no better if we do.

1 CORINTHIANS 10:31

So, if I eat or drink or whatever I do, I do it all for Your glory, God.

COLOSSIANS 2:16-17

Therefore, I will not let anyone judge me by what I eat or drink, or with what I do, in any judgmental way. These are a shadow of the things that were to come; the truth is that nothing satisfies but You, Jesus. True freedom is found in You. Freedom from the bondage of the food restrictions, the religious routines You aren't in, and release from me being my hero. Jesus, where You are, there is *freeeeeeeedom*.

1 TIMOTHY 4:4-5

Everything You created for us to eat is good, and nothing is supposed to be rejected, God, if it is received with thanksgiving because it is consecrated by Your Word and prayer.

A MIRACLE WITH FOOD

LUKE 9:16-17

Taking the five loaves and the two fish and looking up to heaven, You gave thanks and broke them. Then You gave them to the disciples to distribute to the people. The food multiplied, and all the people ate and were satisfied and had more than enough. Then the disciples even picked up twelve basketfuls of extra that were left over!

FELLOWSHIP WITH GOD AND PEOPLE

REVELATION 3:20

There You are! You stand at the door and knock. If anyone hears Your voice and opens the door, You will come in and eat with that person, and they will eat with You.

PSALM 23:5

God, You prepare a table full of amazing food before me in the presence of my enemies for me to sit and work out our differences.

ACTS 2:42

> I devote myself to Your teaching and to fellowship, to the breaking of bread, and prayer.

MATTHEW 6:11

> Give us today our daily bread; I know there is new and fresh spiritual food for me every day!

E

EATING

Chapter 6
FAVOR

I wrote a song about this topic. Here are the lyrics:

> Favor makes you go up, up, up to the top
>
> Up, up, up to the top
>
> You can't earn it
>
> You might not deserve it
>
> But favor makes you go up!

Favor is this extra extension of kindness that is not expected or necessary. It's really cool. Three stories in the Bible come to mind where God extended favor: Esther, Joseph, and Daniel.

ESTHER

Esther has an entire book written about her in the Bible! If you are unfamiliar with her story, she was not a likely choice to be queen according to the cultural perspective of the day. My guess is that many of the girls standing next to her with pedigree, pomp, and circumstance were probably having a hard time hiding their surprised faces when her name was called to go into the time of preparation to become queen. You know those moments when everyone pretends to be super excited for each other at the beauty pageant, but it seems like it's a tad passive-aggressive? I wonder if this was a shock-of-the-century moment or if fake smiles were all the rage back then.

Years prepared Esther. God knew her character. He knew that she would face a moment when she would need to be bold to risk her life and go before the king and stand up to racial injustice on behalf of her people! God knew what was ahead for her and that she was equipped for what she was facing in the palace. God knew she would do what He needed her to do!

So when the time was right, she was chosen because of what was in her, but she was also gorgeous, which didn't hurt. She went and became more of what she was and developed more of what she had with that team of experts. She was beautiful, and God needed her to become more refined and prepared to go before the king. The king could have any woman he wanted, but she was the one the king chose. Esther was who God positioned because God knew what was in her and that she could handle the assignment that would be put on her. *But it takes years to prepare for what looks like an instant change.*

JOSEPH AND HIS BROTHERS

The story of Joseph and his brothers in the Bible is also an intriguing one to me (see Genesis 37-50). I think about how Joseph was perhaps not wise to brag to his family about the dreams God placed in his heart, telling them they were going to bow down to him as he recounted what he saw about the stars and the moon. The story also mentions that he was his father's favorite son, and his dad sealed this deal and made it public with a sought-after colorful robe Joseph wore in front of them. These things aren't the best moves for a guy God wants to put in the palace. Then we watch Joseph on this rollercoaster ride that prepares him with faith and patience and positions him for that prestigious position.

It took time to get Joseph ready for leadership—to help him gain wisdom and to grow the fruit of patience. But in a moment, he was catapulted from the prison to the palace. He had suffered in secret. He was sold into slavery by his brothers. He didn't know this, but they took his special coat that they were jealous of and covered it with animal blood and told their dad he had died! His father didn't know to send a team to look for him. Then his brothers were the very crew that sold Joseph to some Ishmaelites, who then sold him to Potiphar's house. This was a part of the great positioning to get him to the palace down the road, but Joseph did not know that at the time!

He was then put in charge of Potiphar's household. Potiphar was one of Pharaoh's officials. Then Joseph was falsely accused by Potiphar's wife of coming on to her, but really she was mad because he rejected her advances! Potiphar handled it by throwing Joseph in jail! But God was working on Joseph's behalf and saw the whole thing. Joseph was promoted even in jail! This guy kept finding his way to the top. His brothers didn't know any of this was going on, and his dad this whole time thought he was gone forever!

Then two guys he was in jail with, the former baker and the cupbearer for the Pharaoh, had dreams and heard Joseph could interpret them. He said yes! He listened and was able to give both of them an answer. The cupbearer was going to be out of jail soon, and Joseph asked for him to remember him when he was out of there! Seven years later . . .

It turns out Joseph's interpretations came true!

Pharaoh had a dream that needed to be interpreted, and several people tried so many things to figure out his dream but to no avail. Pharaoh was frustrated! Then the cupbearer remembered Joseph and how he could interpret dreams! Quickly they went and got him from jail (after he got cleaned

F

FAVOR

up and prepared to go before the king), and just like that—*just like that*—Joseph went from sleeping on a jail bed to standing before the most powerful man in his part of the world.

Pharaoh was desperate and anxious to see if Joseph could help. He shared his dream, and Joseph interpreted it, and quickly Joseph went from obscurity to second in command. Sad to say, Joseph was right in his processing of the dream! It was intense!

Pharaoh put Joseph in charge of overseeing the plan. As Joseph interpreted this extremely intricate dream, Pharaoh decided to trust the man who knew what God was saying. It was all about storing up food to feed the people in a time of crisis, so Pharaoh said, "Okay, do what God has spoken to you!" Not only did God reposition Joseph and promote him, but He also vindicated and validated him!

Then, during the famine, Joseph's brothers came in to get food for their family from Pharaoh's second-in-command, having no idea it was their brother who had been promoted. (My guess is that it was because of all of the Egyptian make-up and because the last they knew, they had *sold him* to the *Ishmaelites;* so this plot twist was a journey they *could in no way have anticipated!*)

God used Joseph in this highly profound way, and he had been guarding his heart to keep it right and tight, so he was harboring no offense. He reunited with them; his dad was shocked he was alive. He was sweet to his brothers. God ended up using him to provide food for his family in a time of crisis because part of the dream was about storing up food in famine. He *forgave them all,* and it's a powerful story of redemption and favor from his brand-new seat of influence! Very wild turnaround!

DANIEL

Let's look at the life of Daniel. King Darius ordered that no one could pray to any god for 30 days unless it was to him. Daniel was not willing to stop praying to his God. He continued to do so and then was thrown into a den of hungry lions (see Daniel 6). Supernaturally, they did not eat him. When he was alive in the morning, King Darius was shocked and decreed, "We will all now serve the God of Daniel," because it was so impressive to him! What was meant for his harm and destruction launched him into the right spot! A place of honor.

Devotion brings promotion. This doesn't mean you earn your right to the top by listening to the right things, being on good behavior, and looking good on paper. Nice try. Been there, done that. It doesn't work. I think that grosses God out. I have learned that He cares more about our devotion than our acts of righteousness. The pure heart stuff when no one is watching—like when you don't talk back or talk behind someone's back, even when you feel hurt, rejected, and justified. When you aren't judgmental or when you realize there is more to every story than what you see and refuse to sit in the seat of the scoffer and instead cover someone with love. When you leave a place better than you find it. When you take care of people and do unto the least of these as though you're doing it unto God. It's all from a clean heart that a pure stream of love can flow. Devotion equals promotion. Man, this is exciting stuff.

When I started looking at God on a new level and giving Him my utter devotion, I became less judgmental and more loving. There was less of me and more of God—for real—when no one was watching. Then it started to bubble out of my life, and people could see the crystal-clear look in my eyes. The joy of my salvation permeated from my very core.

That relationship with God is where the favor comes from. He's the author and the finisher of our faith. That means He wrote the plan for my life; He started it, and He will finish it. Psalm 139:16-18 says, "Your eyes saw my unformed body; all the days ordained for me were written in Your book before one of them came to be. How precious to me are Your thoughts. How vast is the sum of them. Were I to count them, they would outnumber the grains of sand—when I awake, I am still with You."

So, God, I say that what You say is what I say. I want Your plans and purposes to come to pass in my life, in my days, in my heart—Your thoughts, Your will, not my thoughts or my will.

He knows what His plans and purposes are for us. We can look to Him and trust Him to bring them to completion in our lives. I say every day, "I agree with You, God! Have Your way! Make a way where there is no way! On earth, as it is in heaven!"

When God promotes, He does it on a big scale, and our understanding can be so limited. I am learning not to limit God. I stopped telling God how to do things. I started saying, "Have Your way! Do what You want here!" Sounds simple, but now I say, "Your will and not my own!"

SCRIPTURES USED IN THIS SECTION

"We do not want you to become lazy, but to imitate those who through faith and patience inherit what has been promised."

—HEBREWS 6:12

"How blessed is the man who does not walk in the counsel of the wicked, Nor stand in the path of sinners, Nor sit in the seat of scoffers!"

—PSALM 1:1

"The King will reply, 'Truly I tell you, whatever you did for one of the least of these brothers and sisters of mine, you did for me.'"

—MATTHEW 25:40

"Looking unto Jesus, the author and finisher of our faith, who for the joy that was set before Him endured

the cross, despising the shame, and has sat down at the right hand of the throne of God."

—HEBREWS 12:2, NKJV

"Restore to me the joy of your salvation and grant me a willing spirit, to sustain me."

—PSALM 51:12

"Being confident of this, that he who began a good work in you will carry it on to completion until the day of Christ Jesus."

—PHILIPPIANS 1:6

"Yet not what I will, but what you will."

—MARK 14:36B

A PRAYER ON FAVOR

The Bible says I'll find favor with God and man if I wrap kind-
ness and truth around my neck
I do my best with both of those things
I am standing for the floodgates of blessing to rain down on
me, on my household, on my projects and my whole family
What I put my hand to will prosper and that's for sure
No more wondering about what I am doing this thing for
Advancement, I say! From the east to the west
When You put it in motion, I know it's the best
I open my mouth wide, and You fill it right up
Blessings come to my house and my storehouse erupts
It overflows with so much, I cannot contain it
Because your favor is on me, I just can't explain it!
I'm blessed in the city
I'm blessed in the field
I'm living this favor life out for real
Don't worry, I know how this thing works
I'm not expecting a life with unending perks
I know I have to hold up my end of the deal
Co-laboring, showing up, and keeping it real
But, God, You are full of mercy and grace
And You *bless* Your kids and put a smile on our face
So we are asking for favor, like Joseph and Esther
He was second in command; and the king, he blessed her
I am trusting You for that biblical swag
For that supernatural favor like that, the two of them had
You go before me with blessings like a shield
God, to You my entire life I yield
You make a way where there is no way

So I look to You and give You this day!

It comforts me that You are my rear guard

When I rely on You, life isn't so hard

I mean, yes, there are things I do not expect

But with You I get through without any regret

SCRIPTURES USED IN THIS PRAYER

"Let love and faithfulness never leave you; bind them around your neck, write them on the tablet of your heart. Then you will win favor and a good name in the sight of God and man." **—PROVERBS 3:3-4**

"'Bring the whole tithe into the storehouse, that there may be food in my house. Test me in this,' says the LORD Almighty, 'and see if I will not throw open the floodgates of heaven and pour out so much blessing that there will not be room enough to store it.'" **—MALACHI 3:10**

"Now his master saw that the LORD was with him and how the LORD caused all that he did to prosper in his hand." **—GENESIS 39:3, NASB1995**

"Your descendants will be like the dust of the earth, and you will spread out to the west and to the east, to the north and to the south. All peoples on earth will be blessed through you and your offspring." **—GENESIS 28:14**

"I am the LORD your God, who brought you up out of Egypt. Open wide your mouth and I will fill it." **—PSALM 81:10**

"Then your barns will be filled to overflowing, and your vats will brim over with new wine." **—PROVERBS 3:10**

"Blessed shall you be in the city, and blessed shall you be in the field." **—DEUTERONOMY 28:3, ESV**

"For we are co-workers in God's service; you are God's field, God's building." —**1 CORINTHIANS 3:9**

"But You, O Lord, are a God merciful and gracious, Slow to anger and abundant in lovingkindness and truth." —**PSALM 86:15, NASB1995**

"Therefore the LORD waits to be gracious to you, and therefore he exalts himself to show mercy to you. For the LORD is a God of justice; blessed are all those who wait for him." —**ISAIAH 30:18, ESV**

"So Pharaoh said to Joseph, 'I hereby put you in charge of the whole land of Egypt.' Then Pharaoh took his signet ring from his finger and put it on Joseph's finger. He dressed him in robes of fine linen and put a gold chain around his neck. He had him ride in a chariot as his second-in-command, and people shouted before him, 'Make way!' Thus he put him in charge of the whole land of Egypt." —**GENESIS 41:41-43**

"Now the king was attracted to Esther more than to any of the other women, and she won his favor and approval more than any of the other virgins. So he set a royal crown on her head and made her queen instead of Vashti." —**ESTHER 2:17**

"Surely, LORD, you bless the righteous; you surround them with your favor as with a shield." —**PSALM 5:12**

"This is what the LORD says—he who made a way through the sea, a path through the mighty waters." —**ISAIAH 43:16**

"But you will not leave in haste or go in flight; for the LORD will go before you, the God of Israel will be your rear guard." —**ISAIAH 52:12**

"For the Scripture says, 'Whoever believes in Him will not be disappointed.'" —**ROMANS 10:11, NASB1995**

PERSONALIZED SCRIPTURE DECLARATIONS FOCUSED ON FAVOR

GENESIS 39:4

God, I want favor like Joseph had when You gave him popularity in Egypt. Potiphar put him in charge of his household, and he entrusted to Joseph's care everything he owned. I know *You* did that! You equipped him for the service You needed him to do! God, You turned around what the enemy strategically meant for harm, and You used it to catapult him into his destiny. I am asking for favor like that.

LEVITICUS 26:9

Thank You, God, that You look on me with favor and make me fruitful so I can keep increasing. You keep Your covenant with me.

1 SAMUEL 2:26

I have favor with You, God, and people. Thank You that it's increasing every day, and You are constantly improving my reputation.

2 SAMUEL 2:6

Lord God, You show me kindness and faithfulness, and now I offer favor to others because of the favor You give to me.

PSALM 45:12

Because You favor me, people bless me and are constantly giving me gifts! When they see me, they want to give me things!

PSALM 84:9

Look in my direction, God! Show me Your favor! You are my shield!

PSALM 84:11

You are my shield and sun; You shower me with favor and honor. You don't keep a good thing away from those who walk upright.

PSALM 90:17

God, may Your favor rest on me, and will You establish the work of my hand! I look to *You* to make the way for my success.

PSALM 102:13

God, thank You that the time of Your favor is here; Your appointed time to show favor to me has come. I receive it now! Do what only You can do!

PROVERBS 3:4

Thank You, God, that I have favor and a good name in Your sight and in the sight of everyone!

LUKE 2:52

I am growing in wisdom, stature, and favor with God and people, just like Jesus did while He was on earth.

2 CORINTHIANS 6:2

God, You said that in the time of favor, You heard me, and in the day of salvation, You helped me. I say *now* is the time of Your favor and *today* is the day of salvation!

JAMES 4:6

I humble myself before You, God; I am so grateful You give me grace. I refuse to be prideful because I know that You resist the proud, but You give grace to the humble.

1 PETER 5:5

I yield myself to the people who are my elders and to those in authority over me. I know You oppose the proud and show favor to the humble. I clothe myself with humility, and because of this, I receive Your favor, my God.

Chapter 7
GLORY

I grew up on the front row of church and got to see some be-hind-the-scenes of lives getting changed. One morning I got there early and met a woman with alcohol on her breath. She was tightly squeezed against the back wall. Maybe she felt ashamed. Maybe she was out all night. Maybe she drank before coming. I knew this beautiful woman was why Jesus died on the cross, and she had probably overcome a lot just to be there. I watched God meet her in that building. Over time as she kept coming, I watched her walls fall, and her life transform.

I've watched my dad leave lots of dinner tables to go to hospital calls, and I grew up peering out of the back window, watching him as he comforted people on the side of the road; he was frequently the first on the scene of horrific car crashes. We would wait for ambulances to come as my dad would bring comfort and Jesus in the in-between moments of our lives growing up. My mom also did this to the people on the way. To the lady at the store, when we were getting food, everywhere we went, my parents were bringing the love of God with them on their way to their normal day.

I remember our car hydroplaning and my brother Taylor and I spinning in the backseat, and my parents screaming the name of Jesus, and it felt like the car stopped in midair. Basically, what I have learned is that the glory of God cannot be contained in the walls of the church.

I thought I was close to God. But this last year, something changed. My relationship with God entered a new place. The coolest thing is that God is no respecter of persons. That's sort of a weird way to say we are all equal, and He has more for all of us. Seek God, and you will find Him! Ask, and you will receive! If you want Him, you can have Him! It is so cool! What is so amazing to me about the glory of God is that it's all around us and increases as we are intentional about being closer to Him!

It's about what you are looking at. Feast your eyes on God's promises. Look at His goodness. Seek first His kingdom, His righteousness. Be unlike any other. Be like a tree that is planted by streams of living water that yields its fruit in season! Be ready for Him, looking for Him, waiting for Him; He is there looking for those He can strongly support. Most people are filling up on other things all day. In a world where being distracted seems completely normal, be captured by the love of God. He is more than enough. This is where the glory of God likes to hover. At least, that's what I'm learning.

SCRIPTURES USED IN THIS SECTION

"Then Peter opened his mouth and said: "In truth I perceive that God shows no partiality."

—ACTS 10:34, NKJV

"You will seek me and find me when you seek me with all your heart."

—JEREMIAH 29:13

"Ask, and it will be given to you; seek, and you will find; knock, and it will be opened to you. For everyone who asks receives, and he who seeks finds, and to him who knocks it will be opened."

—MATTHEW 7:7, NKJV

"Come near to God and he will come near to you."

—JAMES 4:8A

"The eye is the lamp of the body. If your eyes are healthy, your whole body will be full of light."

—MATTHEW 6:22

"Trust in the Lord, and do good; Dwell in the land, and feed on His faithfulness."

—PSALM 37:3, NKJV

"But seek first his kingdom and his righteousness, and all these things will be given to you as well."

—MATTHEW 6:33

"That person is like a tree planted by streams of water, which yields its fruit in season and whose leaf does not wither— whatever they do prospers."

—PSALM 1:3

"For the eyes of the Lord range throughout the earth to strengthen those whose hearts are fully committed to him.

—2 CHRONICLES 16:9A

G

GLORY

A PRAYER ON GLORY

I want to see Your glory on the earth manifest in the highest

As Your Word said, I would, if I believe I am not pious

Religion can be good if it's not just routine

But this is all about a heart thing for me

I'm searching for a greater truth

Looking for Your deeper meaning

I don't want to stay on the surface

Where everything is just so shallow seeming

I want to break into the depths, to go where angels are bold to enter

Where the glory of God fills the hemisphere and You're truly at the center

I'm not interested in playing dress-up, playing pretend, playing a game

For the depths, for the truth, for all of You is why I came

I've seen the ones hurting inside come and go in pieces

I've seen Your people misrepresent how You'd want them treated

But what made me stay and has kept me near is knowing Your very heart

That when I get close to You; I know You give people a brand-new start

You really meet people where they are at and love them for who they are

You aren't impressed by status. You're not looking at their car

Your eyes penetrate the deepest place, past the smoke and mirrors

Nothing can be put on for You—You even keep our tears

You love us so much—even in our mess—then You go get the mop

You start cleaning us up in our self-righteousness and love us until we stop

It's Your glory, God, that I want to see; it's Your glory that I want to hear

It's You, God, every day of the week; it's You, that's why I'm still here

SCRIPTURES USED IN THIS PRAYER

"Who among the gods is like you, LORD? Who is like you— majestic in holiness, awesome in glory, working wonders?" **—EXODUS 15:11**

"[B]ut let it be the hidden person of the heart, with the imperishable quality of a gentle and quiet spirit, which is precious in the sight of God." **—1 PETER 3:4, NASB1995**

"For the earth will be filled with the knowledge of the glory of the LORD as the waters cover the sea." **—HABAKKUK 2:14**

"Therefore, if anyone is in Christ, the new creation has come: The old has gone, the new is here!" **—2 CORINTHIANS 5:17**

"But the LORD said to Samuel, 'Do not consider his appearance or his height, for I have rejected him. The LORD does not look at the things people look at. People look at the outward appearance, but the LORD looks at the heart.'" **—1 SAMUEL 16:7**

"You have taken account of my wanderings; Put my tears in Your bottle. Are they not in Your book?" **—PSALM 56:8, NASB1995**

"All of us have become like one who is unclean, and all our righteous acts are like filthy rags; we all shrivel up like a leaf, and like the wind our sins sweep us away." **—ISAIAH 64:6**

"Then Moses said, 'I pray You, show me Your glory!'"
—EXODUS 33:18, NASB1995

"Surely God is my help; the Lord is the one who sustains me."
—PSALM 54:4

PERSONALIZED SCRIPTURE DECLARATIONS TO EMPHASIZE GOD'S GLORY

EXODUS 15:11

Lord, there is no one else like You! You're majestic in holiness, awesome in glory, and You work wonders!

1 KINGS 8:11

I am asking for Your glory to fill all the areas of my life.

1 CHRONICLES 16:24

God, I declare Your glory among the nations and Your marvelous deeds among Your people! Be glorified and magnified on the earth now and forever.

1 CHRONICLES 29:11

God, I magnify You above all else. You are high and exalted. You are worthy to be praised. I put You way above myself and my surroundings, for sure above the distractions and cares I am facing. To You be all the honor, praise, glory, exaltation, and authority in my life. To You be the kingdom; I give You the highest place. I put You above everybody else! You are head over all! You rule, and You reign, and I worship You!

PSALM 3:3

My God and my King, You are a shield all around me and for my household and the ones I love! You are my glory, the one who lifts my head high! I look to You, and I give praise!

G

GLORY

PSALM 8:1

God, Your name is so majestic! I praise You and lift Your name above all other names; be exalted in all the earth! You have set Your glory in the heavens. You have been loyal to a thousand generations; I *know* You are going to see me through (Deuteronomy 7:9). When I feel overwhelmed, I love to think about that, and it brings me great comfort. You can be trusted.

PSALM 29:2

God, today I give You the glory You deserve; I worship You with all of my heart! I give You the highest praise.

PSALM 97:6

The heavens proclaim Your righteousness, God, and everybody sees Your glory!

PSALM 102:15

Lord, You said that the nations will fear Your name; all the kings of the earth will reverence Your glory!

PSALM 104:31

May Your glory endure and remain forever, Lord; may You rejoice in Your works on the earth in great display!

PSALM 105:3

I glorify Your holy name; I rejoice and seek Your face day and night!

PSALM 106:47

Save us, God, and gather us from the nations. Thank You, God, for everything that You've done and everything that You're working on, even when I can't see it! We praise You and revel in Your praise.

PSALM 108:5

God, I put You above everything else in my life, even high above the heavens. I ask for Your glory to cover over all the earth.

PSALM 113:4

God, I exalt You above the nations; Your glory is above the heavens.

PSALM 115:1

Not to us, Lord, not to us, but Your name be all the glory, honor, and power! I exalt You high and lift You up above all else because of Your love and faithfulness.

PSALM 138:5

Your glory is so magnificent; I sing of Your ways!

PSALM 145:11

Lord, I tell of Your glory and of Your kingdom, and I speak about Your power!

Chapter 8

HEALING

By simply watching our bodies respond to a cut, we see how God feels about healing. As soon as we get hurt, our bodies go into overtime to heal, which is impressive proof of God's desire to set healing in motion. I think there is a lot more to healing than we know. We aren't simply skin and bones; we are layered beings, and we need healing in all of our dimensions.

What I have learned in the process of being healed is that it feels vulnerable. You have to let people into your life to see and evaluate the wound and assess what you are dealing with to determine what kind of help you need going forward. That process can be grueling but necessary. So much of the battle of wellness is in your head. If you start to believe you are sick and you take that on as your identity, as in you gain attention for it, it starts to serve you; why get well?

I remember when I was covered in hives, a doctor looked into my eyes as if he was searching my soul, and I asked what he was looking for. He said, "I want to know if you want to get well."

I couldn't believe the doctor was questioning if I wanted to stay sick or not, but the truer part of me loved the deeper evaluation. That part of me stepped right in and said, "Yes,

I do!" Good thing I was raised by parents who didn't coddle illness; otherwise, I'd be a real Ferris Bueller. I'm a dramatic personality, but in my family, you don't get comforted for being sick. You want to move forward ASAP. It's so interesting how in order to get healed, you have to know what is actually going on with you. You have to face off with the situation and be willing to invite someone in and expose the issue. Sometimes, this is embarrassing. You need to get help, and you need to expose your problem to get it fixed.

"And they overcame him by the blood of the Lamb and by the word of their testimony, and they did not love their lives to the death." (Revelation 12:11, NKJV).

What in the world does that mean? Let's dive in.

- "We overcome"—What does it mean to overcome? We get the victory. Breakthrough. Experience a turning point that provides relief in our circumstances finally.
- "By the blood of the Lamb"—Jesus, God's Son, is known as the Lamb. His blood is one of the most potent forces on the planet because it is healing, and in this context, it is being referred to as a sacrificial symbol: "the blood of the lamb."
- "Word of our testimony"—In the Old Testament, the ancient prophets talked about the power of remembrance. Several times this is referred to like when people pulled up rocks from the Jordan River. I've heard they marked scenes on their staff of victories they won with God so they wouldn't forget. Also, there is so much power in the word of our story and what we tell ourselves on so many levels. On the spiritual level, the Bible says this:
  - "For as he thinks in his heart, so *is* he." (Proverbs 23:7a).
  - "We seemed like grasshoppers in our own eyes, and we looked the same to them" (Numbers 13:33b).

- "'Have faith in God,' Jesus answered. 'Truly I tell you, if anyone says to this mountain, 'Go, throw yourself into the sea,' and does not doubt in their heart but believes that what they say will happen, it will be done for them. Therefore I tell you, whatever you ask for in prayer, believe that you have received it, and it will be yours'" (Mark 11:22-24).
- "If you declare with your mouth, 'Jesus is Lord,' and believe in your heart that God raised him from the dead, you will be saved" (Romans 10:9).

I also know this is a highly personal subject for a lot of people. My personal experience through healing has been an interesting one. It's taken a team of people, persistence, faith, and soul-searching lifestyle changes, but Jesus gets all the credit and glory for it. I know that taking care of my body is part of my responsibility. God is the one who knows what we need to do to take care of ourselves the best, but we need to do the daily work.

SCRIPTURES USED IN THIS SECTION

"So Joshua called together the twelve men he had appointed from the Israelites, one from each tribe, and said to them, 'Go over before the ark of the LORD your God into the middle of the Jordan. Each of you is to take up a stone on his shoulder, according to the number of the tribes of the Israelites, to serve as a sign among you. In the future, when your children ask you, "What do these stones mean?" tell them that the flow of the Jordan was cut off before the ark of the covenant of the LORD. When it crossed the Jordan, the waters of the

H

HEALING

Jordan were cut off. These stones are to be a memorial to the people of Israel forever.'"

—**JOSHUA 4:4-7**

"Do you not know that your bodies are temples of the Holy Spirit, who is in you, whom you have received from God? You are not your own."

—**1 CORINTHIANS 6:19**

A PRAYER ON HEALING

I am healed and whole and my body is restored
I put my hope and trust in the Lord
I do not worry; I do not fear
I know that God's healing power is here
Every part of me down to my heart
Knows just what to do, knows just where to start
So I'm not going to shake in my torment all day
I'm not staying the same, heck no, no way
Mind, will, emotions, come in line with my spirit
If you are freaking me out, then I don't want to hear it
So I pray for wisdom, so I can listen to the truth
And I know what I actually need to do
I know my health is really between You and me
I pray for wisdom on the doctors as they are treating me
You know what I should do, so lead my steps today
You created my body and see the path I should take
I will not quit or back down from my fight
So I'll do what You say to make my health right
Sometimes it's been scary and I've felt alone
But I know You're the one who created the moon
You're the author and the finisher and know right from wrong
You know exactly what is going on
So I trust You, God, to know what changes I need to make
And I'll walk it out, the steps to health I should take

SCRIPTURES USED IN THIS PRAYER

"But He was wounded for our transgressions, He was bruised for our iniquities; The chastisement for our peace was upon Him, And by His stripes we are healed." **—ISAIAH 53:5, NKJV**

"For you, O Lord, are my hope, my trust, O LORD, from my youth." **—PSALM 71:5, ESV**

"So do not fear, for I am with you; do not be dismayed, for I am your God. I will strengthen you and help you; I will uphold you with my righteous right hand." **—ISAIAH 41:10**

"Call to me and I will answer you and tell you great and unsearchable things you do not know." **—JEREMIAH 33:3**

"And we all, who with unveiled faces contemplate the Lord's glory, are being transformed into his image with ever-increasing glory, which comes from the Lord, who is the Spirit." **—2 CORINTHIANS 3:18**

"May God himself, the God of peace, sanctify you through and through. May your whole spirit, soul and body be kept blameless at the coming of our Lord Jesus Christ."
—1 THESSALONIANS 5:2.

"If any of you lacks wisdom, you should ask God, who gives generously to all without finding fault, and it will be given to you." **—JAMES 1:5**

"The Lord makes firm the steps of the one who delights in him." **—PSALM 37:23**

"For you created my inmost being; you knit me together in my mother's womb." **—PSALM 139:13**

"Therefore I do not run like someone running aimlessly; I do not fight like a boxer beating the air. No, I strike a blow to my body and make it my slave so that after I have

preached to others, I myself will not be disqualified for the prize." —**1 CORINTHIANS 9:26-27**

"God made two great lights—the greater light to govern the day and the lesser light to govern the night. He also made the stars." —**GENESIS 1:16**

"Looking unto Jesus, the author and finisher of our faith, who for the joy that was set before Him endured the cross, despising the shame, and has sat down at the right hand of the throne of God." —**HEBREWS 12:2, NKJV**

"Who can fathom the Spirit of the LORD, or instruct the LORD as his counselor? Whom did the LORD consult to en-lighten him, and who taught him the right way? Who was it that taught him knowledge, or showed him the path of understanding?" —**ISAIAH 40:13-14**

"Trust in the LORD with all your heart and lean not on your own understanding; in all your ways submit to him and he will make your paths straight." —**PROVERBS 3:5-6**

PERSONALIZED SCRIPTURE DECLARATIONS TO PRAY ABOUT HEALING

EXODUS 23:25

Because I worship You, my God, and put You above everything else in my life, Your blessing will be on my food and water. You will take away sickness from me.

2 KINGS 20:5

I am fully convinced that You have heard my prayer and have seen my tears, and I *know* I am healed, spirit, soul, and body.

2 CHRONICLES 7:14

We, Your people, who are called by Your name, humble ourselves, pray, seek Your face, and turn from our wicked ways, and we know that when we do that, You hear from heaven, and You forgive our sin and heal our land.

PSALM 30:2

Lord my God, I call to You for help, and I am healed in every way, down to my deepest parts.

PSALM 41:3

Lord, You sustain me, even when I am lying here in the darkest moments of confusion and despair; You have always been and always will be here. You restored me from the bed of illness I was in! You restored me back to health!

PSALM 103:2-4

I praise You, Lord, with all my soul, and I refuse to forget any of Your benefits. How could I, God? There are so many! You forgive all of my sins, and You heal all of my diseases; God, I am so thankful! You redeem my life from the deep dark hole and crown me with love and compassion.

PSALM 107:19-21

Every time I cry to You in my desperate place, You save me from my trouble. You sent out Your Word, and it healed me; You rescued me from that place of confusion and despair. I give thanks to You, Lord, for many reasons, but one is that Your love never fails and it has no end; another is for the wonderful things You do. You make me feel so loved. You know me and understand me. You are making all things beautiful. Okay, also, while I am at it, *thank You* for *all* you have done for all of humanity. I am so grateful to You! I worship You, praise You, and am in awe of You! You have restored me and have brought me back to life time and time again, and I *always* put all my hope and trust in You and You alone!

PSALM 146:8

Lord, You give blind people their sight back; You lift those who are humble and love those who are in right standing with You, God. And I know we do that by keeping our eyes on You, not straying far from You. And when we do, we repent quickly and get right back on course! You are so faithful to me, God; I love You with my whole heart! You keep me in all my ways. I choose to stay close to You. Show me what You have for me today.

PSALM 147:3

God, thank You that You heal the brokenhearted and bind up their wounds.

PROVERBS 4:20-22

Heavenly Father, I lean in to hear exactly what You are saying. I am listening specifically for Your words. I want to comprehend precisely how You feel about everything. What is on Your heart is what is on my heart. God, do not let Your words out of my sight; keep them within my heart because I know they are life to me and health to my whole body!

PROVERBS 17:22

Lord, You said that a cheerful heart is good medicine, but a crushed spirit dries up the bones. So today, I am asking for a cheerful heart! I am also participating with You in this and doing everything I know to get this!

ISAIAH 53:5

Jesus, You were pierced for my sins and brutalized for the wicked things I would commit before I even did them; it is baffling to me, but the punishment that brought me peace was put on You, and by Your wounds I am healed.

ISAIAH 58:8

Light! Shine bright like when the sun first breaks over the horizon in the morning, and my healing will quickly appear; then Your righteousness will go before me, and Your glory, Lord, will guard me from the front and the back and protect me even from my blind spots!

JEREMIAH 17:14

Heal me, Lord, and I will be healed; when You do it, it is established. On earth, as it is in heaven. Save me, and I will be saved; You are the one I praise. I trust only in You. You are where my hope comes from.

JEREMIAH 33:6

God, You said that You would bring health and healing and that You will heal Your people and let them enjoy abundant peace and security. So I receive that now! Abundantly!

MALACHI 4:2

Lord, You told us that for those who revere and respect Your name, the sun of righteousness would rise with healing in its rays. And they will go out and frolic like well-fed calves.

MATTHEW 9:35

Jesus, thank You that You heal every single disease and sickness and remove it from my body. You also give me wisdom on what I can do to live a healthy life and how I should be living in step with You in this process day by day as I walk it out!

MARK 5:34

My faith is in Your healing power. I am peaceful and free from all suffering.

HEBREWS 12:2

I fix my eyes on You. You are the living God, the author and finisher of my faith; for the joy set before You, You endured the cross, and I want You to know I am forever grateful.

MARK 9:23

For those who believe, all things are possible through You, God!

COLOSSIANS 3:1

I set my affections on things above, not on things of this earth .

LUKE 4:18

Your spirit, Lord, is on me because You have anointed me to proclaim good news to the poor. You have sent me to proclaim freedom for the prisoners and recovery of sight for the blind, to set the oppressed free!

H

JOHN 8:36

The person You set free is uninhibited in every single way! I look to You and cling tightly while I do. I stay close to You, and I don't walk to the right or the left **(Proverbs 4:27)**. I stay within Your reach!

LUKE 8:50

I resist fear; I choose to believe, and I know I am healed. Show me what practical steps to take today to walk in that healing. I believe I receive Your wisdom.

JAMES 5:15-16

I pray in faith, and I am well. The Lord raises me up, and I am forgiven of all sins. I tell someone my sins and come clean and repent for them and pray, and I am healed. I know my heart has to be right before God and man for my prayers to be powerful and effective!

1 PETER 2:24

Jesus, thank You for taking my sins on Your body on the cross so I might die to sin and live for righteousness; by Your wounds, I have been healed. I receive that healing today and every day.

Chapter 9
INFLUENCES

Being mindful of our influences is so important. I've noticed for myself how many things provide direction that I absorb inadvertently. This can be especially alarming when it comes to our subconscious. It's wild how many elements contribute to our surprisingly impressionable point of view and behavior!

This scripture comes to mind: "Above all else, guard your heart, for everything you do flows from it" (Proverbs 4:23). This blows my mind. Wow! Every issue! That's why I endeavor to be intentional with this! I recently asked several of my closest friends how to do this because this is an area where I am always wanting to grow. I am always working on guarding my heart not to become jaded or offended. It is easy to do, especially when it feels justifiable. Guarding my heart with everyone, including the people so dear and so close, isn't easy, but it's worth it! Only you are the keeper of the condition of your heart.

I want God to choose my influences, not my history with a person. Just because you've always been close to someone doesn't mean you're supposed to stay close to them. Just because they live physically close to you or just because they are in convenient proximity doesn't determine your relational trajectory. What does God say? My internet algorithm shouldn't determine my influences. The internet might be speaking too loudly into our lives. We aren't free if we are addicted (speaking for a friend—just kidding). I want God to determine my relationships. So how is that possible? Do we ask Him? I truly believe in asking Him everything. *God, what is on Your heart? Do You want me to be close to this person? Am I supposed to watch this documentary? Today? What do You want me to do today? I want to be in sync with You today. I agree with You on earth as it is in heaven.*

I realize even though people love me, no one besides God is as interested in my life as I am, so I have learned to pray out my days in agreement with Him. I pray out what the Bible says; it's safe there.

God wants that first-place spot. This has always been a fight not to take things on that I shouldn't—fighting for causes or people or this thing or that thing. I am always working on casting all, the whole of my care, on God. What does that mean? To trust God that He is working all things out for my good.

I have been processing the story about how Jesus was able to sleep in the boat when everyone was freaking out during the storm (see Luke 8:22-25). How convicting! I have been an Olympic-level worrier and dweller. I was worrying about things that *might* happen as a form of love. It sounds ridiculous, I'm laughing at myself as I write this, but the amount of time and energy I have forfeited for this labor of "love" is embarrassing. The last time I checked, it had helped *no one*. And I have been exceptionally good at dwelling on the past. I have had a gift at processing—I'll top that with a better word, say, marinating in—conversations I've had. I used to torment myself with replaying and ruminating, but I'm learning this isn't productive. It's not faith. It's not forward progress. It's where I stall out. It's where bottom dwellers go. It's where I go when I want to feast on my fears, not my faith.

When my eyes are on myself, I go there; when my eyes are on Jesus and on what He has done, on what He will do, it brings me perfect peace; when I keep my eyes on Him, I stay there. I retreat into old habits when my eyes are off of Him.

SCRIPTURES USED IN THIS SECTION

"This, then, is how you should pray: 'Our Father in heaven, hallowed be your name, your kingdom come, your will be done, on earth as it is in heaven.'"
—MATTHEW 6:9-10

"Casting all your cares [all your anxieties, all your worries, and all your concerns, once and for all] on Him, for He cares about you [with deepest affection, and watches over you very carefully.]"
—1 PETER 5:7, AMP

"And we know that in all things God works for the good of those who love him, who have been called according to his purpose."
—ROMANS 8:28

"You will keep in perfect peace those whose minds are steadfast, because they trust in you."
—ISAIAH 26:3

I

INFLUENCES

A PRAYER OVER INFLUENCES

So, God, I want to be influenced only by what You think and say
And anyone *You* want to inspire me, not just who is around me in the day
I choose to be intentional with my circles and let You specify
Will You dictate my proximity so it's not just passers-by?
I know I don't have to be close to people to avoid their offense
But I will listen to You and I'll be led in every sense
So here I am; I am open to correction
Every day I am seeking Your direction
I invite You in, even to the influences of my heart
I don't want to just be led by who is around me at my start
I choose to be open to You and to Your choices
I don't want to listen to the wrong voices
I won't let them dictate what I should do
I stop and take a deep breath and *always* remember to ask You!

SCRIPTURES USED IN THIS PRAYER

"May these words of my mouth and this meditation of my heart be pleasing in your sight, LORD, my Rock and my Redeemer." —**PSALM 19:14**

"Whoever loves discipline loves knowledge, but whoever hates correction is stupid." —**PROVERBS 12:1**

"In the morning, LORD, you hear my voice; in the morning I lay my requests before you and wait expectantly." —**PSALM 5:3**

"Teach me to do your will, for you are my God; may your good Spirit lead me on level ground." **—PSALM 143:10**

PERSONALIZED SCRIPTURE DECLARATIONS TO PRAY ABOUT YOUR INFLUENCE AND INFLUENCES

PHILIPPIANS 4:8-9

All the things that are real, pure, right, clean in the heart, lovely, admirable—if anything is excellent or praisewor-thy—*those* are the things I think about. And You, the God of peace, are with me.

PROVERBS 5:1-2

I lean in at the edge of my seat and pay close attention to wisdom and take notes as You speak to me because Your words bring me such deep insight, God so that I may maintain discretion and my lips may preserve Your knowledge.

PROVERBS 6:20-24

With my whole heart, I watchfully keep my Father's com-mands and will not forget or ignore the lessons my mom taught me. I write them on my heart and wear them around my neck. God, when I walk, Your words guide me; when I sleep, they watch over me; when I wake up, they speak to me. Your Word is a lamp to my feet; it is light. Correction and instruction are the way to live, keep-ing me from trouble.

PROVERBS 22:6

I train up my kids and spiritual kids in the way they should go, and even when they are old, they will not turn from it!

PROVERBS 22:24-25

I will not become friends with someone quick to lose their temper. I will not even associate with one who is easily provoked, or I may learn their ways and get myself stuck in the same trap!

PROVERBS 25:15

God, Your Word says that a ruler can be persuaded through patience, and a gentle tongue can break a bone.

MATTHEW 5:13-16

I am the salt of the earth. Set apart and not like the rest of the people on the planet. I am the light of the world. I let my light shine bright in front of others so they can see my good deeds and honor my Father in heaven.

MATTHEW 13:22

I will not be like a seed that falls with the thorns by hearing the scriptures out of the Bible and letting the things that happen in my day worry me so much that they cause me to worry and choke the Word and make it impossible to bear fruit.

ACTS 20:28

I keep a close watch over myself and all the people that the Holy Spirit has entrusted me with.

ROMANS 14:13

I choose to stop judging other people. Instead, I am committed to not putting any stumbling block or obstacle in the way of anyone by what I say or do!

1 CORINTHIANS 15:33

I refuse to be misled because I know that bad company corrupts good character and morals. I am always at the right place, with the right people, at the right time, doing the right thing; this is according to what You are asking me to do, God! I agree with You, and I refuse to be deceived down a slippery slope where one thing leads to another into the sin that so easily entangles me! Help me to take the way of escape that You provide for me, God!

TITUS 2:7-8

In all my ways, I am living my life in a way that could set an example for other people by endeavoring to do the right thing. In my lifestyle, I show integrity, seriousness, and soundness of speech that cannot be fought against so that those who oppose me may be ashamed because they have nothing bad to say about me.

Chapter 10
JUDGMENT-FREE ZONE

Man, as soon as I started to grasp the concept that we will be judged by the same measure we use to judge other people, I decided to do everything I could to *stop judging at all!* Seriously, though! I also know there is always more to every story than what I can see.

I read in the Bible about how Jesus reacted when the woman caught in the act of adultery was thrown in front of Him. His response has healed so many hearts and impacted mine: "Let any one of you who is without sin be the first to throw a stone" (John 8:7b).

They all dropped their rocks and judgments and vanished one by one. Wow! This has echoed in my heart so many times. It's as if I can hear the rocks falling one by one. And the grace and love Jesus showed her is the guide and gauge of how we must operate with each other. I have needed it; I have received it, and I have hopefully passed it on through my own life.

But of course, I, like everyone, have failed in this too. I have judged, gotten into offense, and wanted to take things into my own hands to bring justice of my own when I feel like I have been done wrong or someone I love has been wronged—*especially that!* But when I stand back and let God do it, wow, it is much better than any plans I have for myself.

The whole concept of removing the plank from our eye before we point out the speck in someone else's is to examine ourselves first. Analyze your vast array of things first before critiquing someone else. It helps me to consider myself.

The woman at the well. Jesus, a Jewish man. He asked this Samaritan woman for a drink of water from the well (see John 4:1-42). He tells her everything she has ever done. He knows she has had five husbands and the one she is with isn't her husband. He gains her respect by knowing her story without her telling Him about it. She knew the Messiah was coming. He said, "It's me." Then she went into town and said, "Come see a man who told me everything I ever did."

I love this story. I love Jesus. He did things that the culture says He shouldn't, but these things pierced people's hearts and changed people's paths. He still does. He has changed me and continues to every day. This is my experience. I am so grateful. He is available to anyone who wants Him. I've seen it over and over. He heals, restores, repairs, remodels—there is nothing in the world like Him.

SCRIPTURES USED IN THIS SECTION

"For in the same way you judge others, you will be judged, and with the measure you use, it will be measured to you."

—MATTHEW 7:2

"You hypocrite, first take the plank out of your own eye, and then you will see clearly to remove the speck from your brother's eye."

—MATTHEW 7:5

J

JUDGMENT-FREE ZONE

A PRAYER ON JUDGMENT

Man, I don't pretend to have it all figured out

But I am not here to judge what other people are about

It's true we will be judged by the same measure we judge others

So shouldn't our measure be zero? So we can truly love each other?

Jesus said anyone who hasn't sinned gets to chuck the first stone

And everyone left, they all went home

Besides Jesus, nobody is perfect with a heart that's white as snow

So let's refuse to act like we are better than anyone; let's all choose to grow!

Looking to the right and left makes it hard to focus on our race anyway

When I do that, I stumble and fall and can't keep up my own pace

So I put on my blinders, my focus shields

There has to be a way to help! My heart to You I yield

You are the only one who knows what's going on

Your perspective is the only angle to which I am holding on

When I judge people from my point of view

My eyes have limitations; besides—I leave that job to You

SCRIPTURES USED IN THIS PRAYER

"My heart is not proud, LORD, my eyes are not haughty; I do not concern myself with great matters or things too wonderful for me." —PSALM 131:1

*"Do not judge, or you too will be judged. For in the same way you judge others, you will be judged, and with the measure you use, it will be measured to you." —***MATTHEW 7:1-2**

"When they kept on questioning him, he straightened up and said to them, 'Let any one of you who is without sin be the first to throw a stone at her.' At this, those who heard began to go away one at a time, the older ones first, until only Jesus was left, with the woman still standing there." —**JOHN 8:7, 9**

*"For all have sinned and fall short of the glory of God." —***RO-MANS 3:23**

*"For by the grace given me I say to every one of you: Do not think of yourself more highly than you ought, but rather think of yourself with sober judgment, in accordance with the faith God has distributed to each of you." —***ROMANS 12:3**

*"Then we will no longer be infants, tossed back and forth by the waves, and blown here and there by every wind of teaching and by the cunning and craftiness of people in their deceitful scheming. Instead, speaking the truth in love, we will grow to become in every respect the mature body of him who is the head, that is, Christ." —***EPHESIANS 4:14-15**

*"Therefore, since we are surrounded by such a great cloud of witnesses, let us throw off everything that hinders and the sin that so easily entangles. And let us run with perseverance the race marked out for us, fixing our eyes on Jesus, the pioneer and perfecter of faith. For the joy set before Him he endured the cross, scorning its shame, and sat down at the right hand of the throne of God." —***HEBREWS 12:1-2**

"For though the righteous fall seven times, they rise again." —**PROVERBS 24:16A**

*"Do not judge, and you will not be judged. Do not condemn, and you will not be condemned. Forgive, and you will be forgiven." —***LUKE 6:37**

PERSONALIZED SCRIPTURE DECLARATIONS TO HELP YOU NOT JUDGE

LEVITICUS 19:15

I do not twist justice; I do not show partiality to the poor or favoritism to the rich and famous, but I treat people fairly.

MATTHEW 7:1-2

I do not judge other people because I don't want to be judged. I know that in the same way I judge others I will be judged; and I can go so far as to say that with the measure I use, it will be measured to me! So my measure is *zero*. I am a judgment-free zone!

JOHN 3:17

God, I am so deeply grateful that You did not send Your only Son, Jesus, into the world to condemn the world for our sins but to save the world.

ROMANS 12:16-18

I live in harmony with others. I am not proud, but instead, I walk in humility. I am willing to associate with people of low position. I am not conceited. I do not repay anyone evil for evil. I am careful to do what is right in the eyes of everyone. If possible, as far as it depends on me, I live at peace with the people I encounter.

ROMANS 14:12-13

Since all of us will give an account of ourselves to God, I stop passing judgment on others. That is up to God! Instead, I choose not to put any stumbling block or obstacle in anyone's way.

GALATIANS 6:1

If someone is caught in a sin, because I live by the Spirit, I restore that person gently. But I also watch myself so that I am not tempted.

HEBREWS 4:12-13

God, Your Word is alive and active. Sharper than any double-edged sword, it penetrates even to divide my soul and spirit, joints and marrow; it judges the thoughts and attitudes of my heart. Nothing in all creation is hidden from Your sight. Everything is uncovered and laid bare before Your eyes, and I must give You an account for my life.

JAMES 4:11-12

I do not slander anyone. I do not judge my neighbor.

Chapter 11

KEEPERS OF THE HEART

Offense is such a tricky, tricky trap. You for sure don't know you're in it. Or you feel so incredibly justified—that's why it works so well. It's fascinating. One time I got up in front of my dad's church and told everyone I was unoffendable. I honestly thought I was. What a dumb thing to say! It was like painting a target on myself! Wow! After that, I was presented with all sorts of opportunities to overcome offenses. It was an unintended fascinating social experiment, but it was awful. I also realized that I'm sure I have caused as many offenses as I have overcome.

This topic applies to our lives as leaders, as heads of families, as whatever we are entrusted with, big or small. Everybody is leading somebody. That is why the stakes are so high that we keep our hearts clean. Having honest people who love you and can walk you through overcoming offenses is essential. I don't know what I would do without them. I have intentionally opened the gates of my heart to a handful of people I listen to because I know I will inevitably have blind spots. A blind spot is, by definition, something you don't even know exists, so that is why we need other people to show us that it is there.

Regarding offence, Proverbs 18:19 explains that it is harder to win a person offended than it is to win a strong city. But Jesus will leave 99 sheep to go after one (see Luke 15:4). It seems ridiculous unless you are that one sheep. Have you ever seen the video on YouTube of the shepherd calling his sheep and all the other people trying to do the same, and the sheep don't come until it's their actual shepherd? The sheep know their shepherd's voice.

Being teachable is one of the most significant and powerful forces in the world. God can do anything with you if you are teachable because you can grow.

It also makes you more likable as a person. It's hard to be around people who are stuck in their ways. I had some people in my life who I noticed had "arrived" in their personal growth system at a certain age. I was 16, and I saw that they were no longer advancing. I am forever grateful to them because, at that moment, my eyes were opened to personal growth and advancement. No, not in the trend sense but in the deepest door of my heart. I did not want to stop growing until the day I died as an old lady. I saw that their maturity capped off and that it was a choice. I decided I would do whatever it took at whatever cost to grow. I would hunt for my blind spots and surround myself with truth-tellers. I would allow the world around me to be my teacher, and I would become the person God intended for me to be.

Now when I go to hire someone, my *number-one* trait is teachability. I can do anything with someone who is willing to grow.

Even on a social and emotional-development level, being willing to meet eye-to-eye with your actual behaviors is the beginning of true change. It's so cool to be in a place where we are not conditioned by what we should believe but in a place where we think for ourselves. Who wants to be a robot walking through the world looking, talking, and speaking like everyone around us when we can be individuals? Not me! How can we do this?

We have to fight for the condition of our hearts. This truly means war. This means you are against people telling you what you believe and making you feel wrong about your morals. This means you fight to keep the walls of offense down, and you get up and love again. I know it's scary—are you kidding me? How can you guard your heart with all diligence but also love your neighbor as yourself? It's sort of like doing the splits in two places. I mean, guarding your heart with all diligence is a part-time job. Be prepared to say "I forgive you" and "I'm sorry" daily because nothing is worth hardening your heart. But I have had layers of coating on me.

I remember a few times I was headed down the road of being a statistic. Just another preacher's daughter, jaded and unsure of people's motives. I remember the phrases rising in me: "This is it?" "This is the thing that took me out?" "Out of all the things I've been through, this was the big battle of impossibility?"

Heck, no!

I would somehow get my fight back. I would refuse to allow all the other tears to be in vain, all the other decisions up to that moment to be for naught. Those times I stood at the crossroads and chose God's will over my own over and over again. Or when I failed and allowed the love and light of God to pick me back up. Was none of that going to count all of a sudden? No way, José.

I've learned that in times of distress, I ask God to help me find my way through it. I also out myself to a friend by ensuring at least one person knows how I feel so I have accountability. Someone knowing where I'm at is always the beginning of change. Well, really, being honest with myself is the *beginning* of change, then telling someone else is the next step. They usually say something like, "You're not going down like this," or "I know you. You're not going to stop here!"

I think to myself, *I'm not? Okay, good. Oh yes, I'm not!* And it gives me the courage not to stay there. I always think it's like going to the gym on that first day; this is the worst of it. It can only get better from here.

So how do we balance guarding our hearts and being vulnerable? That is something I find to be a very interesting line.

I lost my filters when I lived in Nashville. I didn't mean to. To write meaningful songs, in truth, not just plastic wrap but the real stuff, I had to lose the filter. It wasn't just that; it was also facing those things I needed to grow in. Hard times are good to force change if we let them. Nashville was a wonderful and personal development season for sure!

I'm smiling thinking of this one birthday I had. It was an awkward moment when all I wanted to do was have everyone I was with tell me things I could work on to improve. They were horrified. "No, absolutely not!" one of my friends responded at the table. I realized at that moment that they didn't get me. I was at the wrong table. People who challenge me to grow from a place of love are my people. The ones who constantly raise the bar and inspire me to pursue a higher version of myself but in the sweetest way—those are my people. Faithful are the wounds of a friend.

It is scary when the fear of people is on everyone in the room so much that no one tells you the truth. I want genuine love that raises the standard, calls me higher, and won't let me stay in offense! I left the table. I got into a different group of friends. It wasn't their fault. It was a great season of friendship, and that moment helped me realize that it was the end of that chapter of my life with those friends.

So I have learned that we all have seasons for things. We need to be at the right place, for the right amount of time, with the right people, doing the right thing.

I have also learned that forgiveness is primarily for the forgiver and a teeny tiny bit for the forgiven. Keeping my heart is my job, and it is not based on what the person in front of me did or did not do. Forgiveness isn't earned; it is a choice. I am not excusing bad behavior; I am just saying we are the gardeners of our hearts. If they don't repent, I still forgive because heavy is the heart that holds a grudge.

In the Bible, Peter asked how many times he needed to forgive someone, and Jesus replied 70 times 7 (see Matthew 18:22). My friend's granny calls someone she knows, who is hard to forgive, her "70-times-7." "Here comes my '70-times-7,'" she will say. A big part of life is forgiving and repenting. I know I have been and probably am at least one person's "70-times-7!" And I, too, have to forgive my "70-times-7." I sure have learned so much from her. It helps me to think about that.

It is so important to forgive. I am still learning how to live this life of balance between guarding my heart against offense and staying open to the right things. I believe we take it one thing at a time. That is a key to me stepping forward on the tightrope of this subject. No broad brushstrokes of internal rules for this one. More like step-by-step checking in with God on how to handle each thing.

SCRIPTURES USED IN THIS SECTION

"Above all else, guard your heart, for everything you do flows from it."

—PROVERBS 4:23

"The second is this: 'Love your neighbor as yourself.' There is no commandment greater than these."

—MARK 12:31

"Now hope does not disappoint, because the love of God has been poured out in our hearts by the Holy Spirit who was given to us."

—ROMANS 5:5, NKJV

"Let us therefore come boldly to the throne of grace, that we may obtain mercy and find grace to help in time of need."

—HEBREWS 4:16, NKJV

"Faithful are the wounds of a friend; profuse are the kisses of an enemy."

—PROVERBS 27:6, ESV

"Then Peter came to Him and said, 'Lord, how often shall my brother sin against me, and I forgive him? Up to seven times?' Jesus said to him, 'I do not say to you, up to seven times, but up to seventy times seven.'"

—MATTHEW 18:21-22, NKJV

A PRAYER TO KEEP YOUR HEART STEADY

God, I will keep my heart with all diligence
Because out of it all issues flow
I won't let myself veer to the right or the left; instead, where
You say, I will go
So many people are flaky and shaky and make me feel like I'm
on the sand
But I look to You and I will stay faithful because I can trust in
Your hand
I'll be a keeper of the hearts You've spotlighted, the ones
You've assigned me to
I won't be neglecting the ones You have left me; I'll be faithful
to You
There are so many others who've grown cold and severe, but
it isn't over for them yet
They can be thawed and defrosted, loved back to life; I've nev-
er seen one You neglect
Your love is unending; big egos start bending when they know
who You truly are
I am so thankful, eternally grateful, that Your saving grace
isn't far
Under Your wings I'm resting, my life I'm investing; with You, I
am peaceful and calm
You are the healer, my only peace dealer; I can trust in Your
soothing balm
With You, I miss nothing; my heart starts thumping; God, You
just can't be beat
I will stay steady, and I remain sure that what You've started
You will complete
You untie the knot and love me for real as I seek You for unction
That's why I sit at Your throne; it's You alone who repairs every
disfunction

125

So I invite You in; let the change begin; I refuse to take on offense

You're my high tower, the one with the power, and I love You in every sense

SCRIPTURES USED IN THIS PRAYER

"Above all else, guard your heart, for everything you do flows from it." —**PROVERBS 4:23**

"Do not turn to the right or the left; keep your foot from evil." —**PROVERBS 4:27**

"I cling to you; your right hand upholds me." —**PSALM 63:8**

"This happened so that the words he had spoken would be fulfilled: 'I have not lost one of those you gave me.'" —**JOHN 18:9**

"Yet I hold this against you: You have forsaken the love you had at first. Consider how far you have fallen! Repent and do the things you did at first." —**REVELATION 2:4-5A**

"The faithful love of the LORD never ends! His mercies never cease." —**LAMENTATIONS 3:22, NLT**

"He will cover you with his feathers. He will shelter you with his wings. His faithful promises are your armor and protection." —**PSALM 91:4, NLT**

"He heals the brokenhearted and binds up their wounds." —**PSALM 147:3**

"A person's wisdom yields patience; it is to one's glory to overlook an offense." —**PROVERBS 19:11**

"The LORD is my rock, my fortress and my deliverer; my God is my rock, in whom I take refuge, my shield and the horn of my salvation, my stronghold." **—PSALM 18:2**

PERSONALIZED SCRIPTURE DECLARATIONS TO HELP YOU BE UNOFFENDABLE

MATTHEW 5:38-42

When people do something evil to me, I don't get back at them myself; I leave that up to You, God! If someone hits me on the right side of the face, I turn to them and offer the left side. And if anyone wants to sue me and even take my shirt, I hand over my coat as well, even my favorite one! If anyone forces me to go one mile, I'll go with them two miles, by choice! I give to the one who asks me, and I do not turn away from the one who wants to borrow from me.

LUKE 17:3-4

I watch myself closely. If someone sins against me, I go to them about it so we can work through it. If they repent, I forgive them! Even if they sin against me seven times in a day and seven times come back to me saying, "I am sorry," I will forgive them!

EPHESIANS 4:1-3

I live a life worthy of the calling I have been given by You, God. I am working with all my heart to be humble, and I am laboring to be gentle. I am doing my best to be patient, and I choose to stay with people through whatever they are dealing with. That is, when it's healthy. I work to remain in a place of love as I hope they work with me in love. I make every effort to keep the unity of the Spirit through the bond of peace.

PROVERBS 27:5-6

I am so grateful when a friend points out the truth and tells me about a blind spot I have, even if it is hard to hear. Open rebuke is better than hidden love. Wounds from a friend can be trusted, but an enemy covers you in meaningless, manipulative kisses.

JAMES 1:19-20

I listen quickly; I don't speak unless I am convinced I am supposed to. And I do not lose my temper fast because human anger does not make me righteous or produce fruit in my life that You desire, God.

2 TIMOTHY 2:24

I am not someone who causes strife on purpose, but instead, I am kind to everyone, able to teach, and not resentful.

2 CORINTHIANS 13:11

I rejoice, and I reach out for full restoration. I encourage other people. I stay in unity, and I live in peace. You are the God of love and peace and are always with me.

ROMANS 12:17-21

I do not pay anyone back when they do an evil thing to me. I am careful to do what is right in the eyes of other people. As much as it depends on me, I live at peace with all people. I do not take revenge into my own hands, but I leave room for God to take care of things. It is His to avenge; He will repay. If my enemy is hungry, I feed him; if he is thirsty, I give him something to drink. In doing this, I heap burning coals on his head. I am not overcome by evil, but I overcome evil with good.

JOHN 13:34-35

God, Your love is everlasting; it never runs out. It's so unique. It's not the same as human love. You love us without merit or boundaries, and it is not based on circumstances. Out of *that* love is what I am committed to love other people with. By this love everyone will know that I am one of Your disciples, Jesus because I love others the way You love me. It's a recognizable love because it is unique, unlike any other. So when I love like You, first of all, it is sustainable and possible to love people who are hard to love and to forgive when it is challenging, but also, there is a different flavor or seasoning to it; it is You, God! It is not human love, but it is *Your* love, God! *That* is how I choose to love.

1 PETER 3:9

I do not repay evil with evil or insult back with another dig. I do the opposite; when someone does something hurtful to me, instead I think of something I can do to express love to them because when I do this, I know I receive a blessing in return.

HEBREWS 12:15

I choose to walk in Your grace, God. I refuse to be bitter and allow a bitter root to grow inside of me and cause trouble because I know that could defile me and impact the lives around me, causing upset in a lot of people's lives! I don't want that! No way am I going to let that happen. So I choose to deal with this offense now at its source by dealing with this head-on! I am not easily offended. Show me how to guard my heart! Give me grace. I quickly forgive!

LEVITICUS 19:18

I do not find a way to get revenge or hold on to any horrible, mean intentions toward anyone; instead, I love my neighbor and the people in the path of my life the same way I love myself, and I treat them in the manner I want people to treat me.

ACTS 24:16

I make a big effort to always keep my conscience clear before You, God, and people too, even when they are challenging my love walk.

MATTHEW 6:14

I forgive other people when they sin against me; You, my heavenly Father, will also forgive me.

COLOSSIANS 3:12-14

I wear compassion, kindness, humility, gentleness, and patience like clothes. I sit with others no matter what is going on; I ride it out unless it is unhealthy for me to be there, but I always forgive them. When other people wrong me, I forgive them. I forgive because You, God, forgave me! How could I not?! When I think about that, it makes it a lot easier! And out of all these virtues, I put on *love*, which binds us all together in perfect *unity*.

1 JOHN 4:21

Because I love You, God, I also love my brothers and sisters.

LUKE 23:34

Just like You, Jesus, I forgive people. I realize they don't know what they are doing when they are hurting me. I want people to forgive me and extend grace and mercy to me when I need it!

K

KEEPERS OF THE HEART

ROMANS 12:14

I bless those who are weird with me; I choose to keep a pure heart. I know that You, God, are working on my behalf. I want people to forgive me, so I live a lifestyle of extending grace and mercy.

EPHESIANS 4:26-27

When I am angry, I choose to hold it together, and I do not sin. I refuse to let the sun go down while I am still mad, and I do not give the devil an open door.

EPHESIANS 4:32

I am kind and show compassion to other people, forgiving people as quickly as I can, just like You, God, forgave me.

1 JOHN 2:10-11

I love my brother and sister and because of this, I live in the light, and there is no offense in me that causes me to stumble.

PROVERBS 4:23

Above everything else, I guard my heart because every single issue of life flows from it.

ROMANS 12:2

I do not conform to the pattern of this world, but I am transformed by renewing my mind. So I choose to fix my mind on You, God, to look at You, to gaze at You, to fix my eyes on You, and meditate on Your Word. I will be able to test and approve what Your will is—Your good, pleasing, and perfect will.

PROVERBS 23:26

Father, I give You my heart and let my eyes delight in *Your* ways.

PSALM 51:10

Create in me a pure heart, my God; maintain a consistent spirit within me.

PSALM 73:26

My mind, will, and emotions may try to quit on me, but *You*, God, are the strength of my heart and my portion forever. *You* are more than enough for me!

PSALM 37:4

I find my joy in You, and You give me the desires of my heart, Lord.

PSALM 9:1

I give thanks to You, God, with all my heart; I just can't help but tell everybody about all the amazing things You do. They spill out of me day and night.

PSALM 26:2

God, will You check me and make sure I don't have anything weird going on inside my heart? If I do, please let me know! I don't want anything between us!

MATTHEW 5:8

I choose to have a pure heart, and because of that, I know I will see You, God.

PSALM 19:14

God, will You help me? I want what I think about all day to please You! You are the King of my life. You are my Lord, my stabilizer, and my redeemer. You pull me from the pit!

K

Chapter 12
LOVE

Love. Love is the most powerful force on earth.

"The love walk" to me is how we flow with other people on a daily basis. "Walking in love" is choosing to see people the way God sees them, through the eyes of the people they are called to be and not how they may or may not be acting right now. Love is choosing to call people higher and treating them how you would if Jesus was watching you. Love is not slandering people when they walk away, not feeding on the daily gossip of people's lives, even if they are "famous." It's not being fake, unkind, or jealous, but instead calling people higher into the person you believe God sees them to be.

To me, the love walk is easy until it's not. It's easy to walk in love when people are lovable, but we get tested when someone is provoking, agitating, manipulative, etc. The love walk doesn't mean you stay in unhealthy relationships or in closer proximity to people than you should be. It's all about loving people the way you want to be loved. Love doesn't mean letting people hurt you, but it does mean you forgive.

Love is what people are supposed to know Christians by, but it is the thing that is attacked the most directly in a person's life. The scripture "treat others how you want to be treated" comes to mind (Luke 6:31, my paraphrase). When I actually think about how I would want to be treated, it's way easier for me to decide how to treat someone else.

This golden rule has become one of the biggest clichés we have as a society. It's so easy to brush off, so hard to implement, so natural to expect, and extremely challenging to employ. When we simplify it and break it down into its finite parts, it makes the infrastructure of our actions and the mechanical nature of what it means to walk in love a simple one, two, three: Do unto others the way you want them to do unto you. When I think about this and apply it to the processes of my heart, it makes my daily choices very clear, straightforward, obvious, and easy.

Why don't we do this every day? Like at the bank? When the person is being so, so rude and wants to close early but isn't telling me it's because her grandma is in the hospital. She cannot verbalize her feelings because she has no emotional development, so therefore no words to articulate her struggle. She is taking out her grief and pressure on me by making me feel like it's somehow my fault. But instead of me, in turn, projecting my frustration out on her, I'll say, "No problem." I'm sure there is more to the story. I can always come back and quickly let her off the hook the way I would want to be.

Or how I was tempted to be rude when the appointment that I was majorly looking forward to (which was exceptionally challenging to get into) was rescheduled. But I realized there was probably a good reason, so I let her off the hook. She appreciated it. Kindness goes a long way. Love is a matter of the heart. Everything starts there. It can be teeming with living water, or it can be a toxic waste zone based on what we fix our eyes on, ponder, process, and meditate on. It determines the nature of the source of our hearts.

We don't have to love people with our own ability to love; we love people with God's ability to love—it's a whole other level of the love walk. It's in Him. It flows through us.

It's so cool. It's not based on merit; it is unconditional love. Looking at mountains or the ocean, or even the moon or the stars, I get a glimpse of the overwhelming love of God. It is so beyond our ability to earn it. He loves us so much. It is truly amazing. I am so grateful that His eye is upon me. How can we grasp His love for us? It is so broad and so deep! I seriously think about how He draws us in! Every one of us. Over and over again. Wow! *How does He do it?!*

I think of the story of Jonah in the Bible. That story deeply encourages me. It shows the extent of the love of God. He was willing to go *so far* as to fight for one man to get back on track so he would do what he was supposed to do. I mean, wow. That blows my mind.

I want to be easy to work with. I realize that when I am not, I have to deal with the consequences of that. But God is not done with us. He doesn't throw us away. He loves us. I have heard people talk about doomsday doctrine. By this, I mean constantly focusing on the negative and how mad at you God is for this and for that. I don't relate. You can have it like that if you want it. But that is not my experience. The closer I get to God, the more I feel His love.

I look at Jesus and see how He changed the life of a man who was dealing with being wicked but was also hungry to know Jesus (see Luke 19:1-10). He climbed the tree to see Jesus, and Jesus invited him to lunch. And the religious people around Him complained, exclaiming, "If You associate with him, we don't want to associate with You." Jesus went to lunch with him anyway.

Let's lean in a little closer to the story.

He boldly took an action of love with a simple but life-changing lunch, and this guy, who was known as an "unscrupulous tax collector" because he stole from all these people, melted before Jesus. He gave them back all he stole from them and more. I think, *What in the world did Jesus say over this lunch?* All I know is that I relate! The more I know Jesus, the more I melt before Him. The closer I am to Him, and the more time I spend with Him, the more this story makes perfect sense. To know Him, to understand Him, is to know His love.

I, along with many people, have been hurt by church misunderstandings. I'm sure I have been the cause of some myself for other people. I remember a season I never knew if I would be my Tigger self again. I didn't even feel like Pooh. I felt straight up like Eeyore in the Hundred Acre Wood. As I was processing the confusion caused by the pain of people coming and going who I thought were my family, I remember saying to someone I trust, "I hate people, and I hate Christians most of all." With eloquence and compassion, they comforted me, saying, "It's not the Christian part that you hate. It's the part that needs God that has been hurtful. The fact that we are all here to serve God is what we have in common, but we are still all in our process of becoming like Jesus."

That clarity helped open my eyes immediately. That was a future-determining moment. I decided to have love and compassion instead of holding on to my loathing and disdain that were growing in the darkness of hurt. Shining a light on what I was thinking about made the offenses scatter as I faced off with them one by one, realizing there was simply more to the story.

I want to be let off the hook, so I extend that same mercy from my heart. I want people to assume the best about me, so I will choose to assume the best about other people. Upon further investigation, I realized, *sheesh*, I am sure I have caused other people to hurt, so there is no need to focus on the bad stuff instead of the good in others. I want to be forgiven. I already have been by God, so I forgive others.

I remember studying the story from the Bible about a woman at a well. (If you don't know it, go check it out! It's in the book of John in chapter four.) This story of compassion, love, understanding, and truth led me to see how much Jesus' love for us is unending. I saw Him for myself again. I keep seeing Him again and again and again. He makes all things new. For me. For the people around me. How could I hold people to the fire of their sin and bind them to the chains as a slave of their actions when Jesus said that he who the Son sets free is free indeed? John 8:36 says, "So if Jesus, God's Son Himself, *sets* you *free*, you will most certainly be *free indeed*" (my paraphrase). Who am I to say or do anything outside of what Jesus does?

Our family friend used to say, "I open up my Bible, and I have a personal revival." Yeah. That's me. That can be you. Our lives are in God, through God, with God, and for God. God, God, God. He is, always has been, and always will be love.

The guide of doing unto others as I want them to do to me has changed me. It sounds so simple, but it isn't easy to apply sometimes. As I endeavor to become more like Jesus, it becomes easier and easier to do this. When I am struggling, and my eyes are on myself or my circumstances, I have to fight for this more. It depends on what I am looking at, feasting on, and filling myself up with. That is what determines how much of a challenge it is to apply.

The scripture about not delighting in evil hit me in the heart. (see 1 Corinthians 4:6). I believe it's so easy to be entertained by other people's mistakes and tragedies. I think it's human nature, or the Bible wouldn't talk so much about keeping our flesh in line in these areas; I love how honest the Bible is. However, I have noticed a shift since I stopped watching the news, TV, and movies. Peace has replaced fear. God's Word has replaced the latest gossip on people who come and go and are not in my life. Our culture has such an obsession with things that matter not! *They do not matter.*

The people matter because they are humans. But not because they are famous. Only God deserves adoration. I stopped looking over there, and my life has been so much better. It's helped me love from a pure stream instead of focusing on lesser things. I still pray for celebrities and people of cultural influence; I just don't feast on the information of their lives for entertainment. I still keep up with what's going

L

LOVE

on in the world by reading the news as needed, but I don't let it fill my head for hours.

Daily shifting my eyes onto Jesus is the transformative habit that keeps my heart in the right place. I spend my time listening to books, creating art, loving on people, and taking care of myself and what I've been entrusted with. I am convinced I consumed more media than anyone I know before this change. Will it be like this forever? I don't know. I watch things occasionally as I feel led to, but entertainment is no longer a companion or space filler in my life. I simply am not interested.

SCRIPTURES USED IN THIS SECTION

"By this everyone will know that you are my disciples, if you love one another."

—JOHN 13:35

"Treat others the same way you want them to treat you."

—LUKE 6:31, NASB1995

"The eyes of the LORD are toward the righteous and his ears toward their cry."

—PSALM 34:15, ESV

"And may you have the power to understand, as all God's people should, how wide, how long, how high, and how deep his love is."

—EPHESIANS 3:18, NLT

"He who was seated on the throne said, 'I am making everything new!' Then he said, 'Write this down, for these words are trustworthy and true.'"

—REVELATION 21:5

"'I am the Alpha and the Omega,' says the Lord God, 'who is, and who was, and who is to come, the Almighty.'"

—REVELATION 1:8

"For God is love."

—1 JOHN 4:8B, NKJV

A PRAYER ON LOVE

The love walk is a journey, and we can't stray from the path
If we get off of the road, then it can be hard to get back
It's easy to do, but man, it's a trap
That is why getting out of love is so bad
What can you do every single day
To walk in love and to not stray
Forgive as soon as possible; it's a 911
Of course, I know this is easier said than done
But this is important, or it can become bitterness or offense
And both ruin your life, so entertaining them doesn't make sense
There's more to every story, of this I'm certain
When you don't walk in love, it's you that you're hurting

SCRIPTURES USED IN THIS PRAYER

"Anyone who loves their brother and sister lives in the light, and there is nothing in them to make them stumble." **—1 JOHN 2:10**

"Let all that you do be done in love." **—1 CORINTHIANS 16:14, ESV**

"Above all, love each other deeply, because love covers over a multitude of sins." **—1 PETER 4:8**

PERSONALIZED SCRIPTURE DECLARATIONS TO GUIDE LOVE

LEVITICUS 19:17-18

God! I love You; I refuse to get into offense or to let things that come up with people get in the way of my relationship with You. I am going to do whatever it takes—*whatever it takes*—to keep my heart pure, right, and clean before You, God! So I forgive and repent daily. I speak honestly, and I don't seek revenge or keep a grudge against anyone, God. I love my neighbor the same way I love myself, so I forgive, forgive, forgive; that's what I want people to do with me.

PROVERBS 3:3-4

I refuse to let love and faithfulness leave me; I wrap them around my neck, and wear them around like a necklace, and I write them on the tablet of my heart. Because of this, I win favor and a good reputation in the eyes of people and in Yours, God.

PROVERBS 10:12

I know that when I have hatred in my heart, it stirs up conflict, but love covers over all wrongs.

PROVERBS 17:17

A friend loves no matter what, and a brother and a sister are both born for our hardest times.

PROVERBS 21:21

I pursue righteousness with all my heart because I love to be in right standing with You! I also pursue love, so I find

L

LOVE

life, prosperity, and honor. I know I get what I look for, so I am looking for You and all the things that matter to You!

MARK 12:30-31

I love You, Lord, my God, with all my heart and with all my soul and with all my mind and with all my strength! There is nothing I withhold from you! *And* I love my neighbor as myself! So I know that means I have to love myself! There is no commandment more significant than these!

JOHN 13:34-35

I follow Your commands, God, and I love other people! The way You love me, I love people in that same way. People will know that I'm Your follower, Jesus, by the love I have for other people. I want to be a reflection of You in all I do.

ROMANS 12:9-10

My love is sincere. I turn away from evil; I cling to what is good. I am devoted to other people in love, and I honor people above myself.

ROMANS 13:8

I am responsible to continually love other people, and by doing this, I am doing what is important to You, God.

1 CORINTHIANS 14:1

I closely follow the way of love with every part of my heart, and I desire gifts of the Spirit, especially prophecy.

1 CORINTHIANS 13:1

If I speak in the tongues of men or angels but do not have love, I am just making a bunch of noise, and my faith doesn't count.

1 CORINTHIANS 16:14

Everything I do, I do in love.

GALATIANS 5:22-23

The fruits of the Spirit are all growing in my life: love, joy, peace, longsuffering, kindness, goodness, faithfulness, gentleness, and self-control.

EPHESIANS 4:2

I humble myself and am gentle. I'm patient; it is easy for me to handle others with care in love.

EPHESIANS 4:32

I am kind and compassionate to other people. When a situation comes up, I think about how I need to handle it; I choose to be forgiving, just how You forgave me of my sins, Jesus. I choose to extend mercy.

EPHESIANS 5:2

I walk in the way of love, just like You loved me, Jesus, and gave Yourself up for me as a fragrant offering and sacrifice to God.

COLOSSIANS 3:12-14

As one of Your chosen people, God, I walk in holiness and am dearly loved by You! I clothe myself with compassion, kindness, humility, gentleness, and patience. I bear with other people and forgive them for anything they do to hurt my feelings, to bait me into offenses. I forgive them as You forgave me. Above all these virtues, I put on love; I know that binds us all together in perfect unity.

1 THESSALONIANS 3:12

Lord, increase and overflow Your love in me and for other people.

1 TIMOTHY 4:12

I don't let anyone look down on me because of my age, but I set an example for the believers in speech, conduct, love, faith, and purity.

2 TIMOTHY 1:7

God, Your Spirit does not make me timid but gives me power, love, and the ability to keep my flesh under submission to my spirit.

HEBREWS 13:1-2

I keep on loving other people around me as brothers and sisters. I treat them with high regard, not based on what they do to or for me. I do not forget to show hospitality to strangers because when I do that, I could be hosting angels without knowing it.

1 PETER 4:8

Above everything else, I love other people deeply because love covers over many sins. I am so grateful for this.

1 JOHN 3:11

This is the message I have heard from the very start: I should love other people, so I do! Help me to love other people the way You do!

L

LOVE

1 JOHN 4:16

I know and rely on Your love, God, and what it has for me. You are love. I live my life in love, so I abide in You, God, and You take habitation in me.

1 JOHN 4:8

Whoever does not love does not know You, God, because You *are* love itself.

1 JOHN 4:11

Since You loved me, God, I can love others.

EXODUS 34:6

God, You are full of compassion and are gracious. You are slow to anger and are abounding in love and faithfulness.

DEUTERONOMY 7:9

I know that You, my God, are the only true God. You are faithful. You keep Your covenant of love to a thousand generations of those who loved You and keep Your commandments.

DEUTERONOMY 10:18-19

God, You defend the cause of the people who have no father and the ones who have lost their spouse, and You love the stranger who lives among us; You give them food and clothes. I love those You love. I love those who are from a faraway land. Because people are close to Your heart, they are close to mine!

1 CHRONICLES 16:34

I give thanks to You, Lord. You are good. Your love never ends; it endures forever and withstands all.

PSALM 36:5-6

Your love reaches to the heavens, Your faithfulness to the skies. Your righteousness is like the highest mountains, Your justice like the great deep. You, God, preserve both people and animals.

PSALM 86:15

You are full of compassion and grace, God; You're slow to anger, and You abound in love and faithfulness.

JEREMIAH 31:3

Thank You for loving me with an everlasting love; You have drawn me with unfailing kindness.

ZEPHANIAH 3:17

My God, You are with me; You are the Mighty Warrior who saves. You take great delight in me. In Your love, You no longer rebuke me, but You rejoice over me with singing.

LUKE 6:35-36

I love my enemies; I do good to them and lend to them without expecting to get anything back. And because I do that, my reward is great, and I am Your child, God! You are kind, even to the ungrateful and wicked. I am merciful, just as You, Father, are merciful.

JOHN 15:9-10

God, the way that You love Jesus is the way He loves me. I remain in that same love.

JOHN 15:12-13

I love others as You have loved me, God. Greater love has no one than this: to lay down our lives for our friends!

ROMANS 8:35-39

Who can separate me from Your love, Jesus? Can going through adversity, hardship, persecution, offense, having nothing to eat, no clothes to put on my back, danger, or even a battle that is worse than what I have mentioned separate me? No, it's the exact opposite! In all these things, I am *more* than a conqueror through You who love me. I am convinced that nothing, not death or life, angels or demons, the present or the future, or any powers, no matter how significant, or anything else in all creation, can separate me from Your love, God, that is in Jesus, who rules and reigns in my life!

1 CORINTHIANS 13:4-8

I am patient. I am kind. I do not envy. I do not brag. I am not full of pride, but I am humble. I do not dishonor other people. I am not seeking my own way. I am not easily angered. I don't keep a list of what other people did wrong to me! Instead, when I am hurt, I forgive them quickly and don't bring it up again. That is what I want done to me! I do not enjoy evil, and I am not entertained by it. Instead, I rejoice with the truth. I always protect. I never stop trusting. I keep hoping; my perseverance is unending through You, God! I do this in Your strength and not my own! God, Your love in me never fails!

EPHESIANS 4:2-3

I walk in complete humility and have a gentle way; I am patient and bear with everyone in love. It comes easy to me to love people; it is my way of life. I make an effort every day to stay in unity and to walk in the Spirit by living a lifestyle of peace.

COLOSSIANS 3:14

I put on love, which binds me together in perfect unity with the right people.

1 JOHN 3:1

God, I see what great love You have poured out on me that I get to be called a child of God! That is what I am!

1 JOHN 4:19

I love You, God, because You first loved me.

1 JOHN 4:21

God, You commanded that since we love You, we should love others, and I say yes to this! Simply because You told me to and because I love You, God, I choose to love others.

Chapter 13
MONEY

The love of money is the root of all evil. I have thought about this a lot. What a wild statement! That is a lot for me to process. That is the basis for all of the evil in the whole world. I mean, *dang!*

But money itself isn't evil; it's just a matter of what people do with it. I find the whole theory of learning how to be abased and how to abound to be an interesting concept. I have a friend who has experienced both plenty and not much, and she told me both have been good. I was surprised and asked her to clarify, and she explained that both present different challenges. One is having fun getting creative by learning to make ramen noodles a million different ways and making date nights out of nothing. And the other is learning how to have a lot; things cost more with a more lavish lifestyle, so that has to be sustained. Also, depending on how they acquired their riches, they have dealt with a variety of obstacles. Both are two different sides of life but offer a variety of things.

I have seen people with plenty who seemed to have bankrupt emotional and spiritual lives. I have walked with people as they proudly showed me their cardboard huts, made of things they gathered as if they were mansions. Wealth is in the hands of the one who is deciding the value. So many people who live in huge houses and have lots of money cry themselves to sleep and wonder who their real friends are because they worry about what people's true motives are. As some parents are chasing dreams of wealth or working to appear wealthy and ending up in a cycle of debt, sometimes their kids become emotional orphans as they grow up more and more isolated.

Money is not evil. However much you have, learn to manage it well. Give it, save it, spend it, tithe it (this is giving ten percent and is a principle rooted in the Christian faith that we give God the first of the fruit of our labor; it has always helped me to think of tithing as a representation of the way I spend my time and how to honor God with my way of life). I also believe in the biblical principle of sowing and reaping in every form. I have heard people from different perspectives sell this point of view, and I have seen it work so many times in my life. People have said that what goes around comes back around. They've called it karma and the law of attraction. I believe people can have money and things as long as the money and stuff doesn't have them.

God isn't into idols, but it sure is easy for things to work to get into that spot between someone and God. Distraction quickly makes us veer from the primary goal. Walking in certain parts of the world has expanded my vision for so many things. Travel opens our eyes to how small and big the world is at the same time. Money can solve big problems as long as it doesn't become a master over the one who is supposed to be responsible for it.

SCRIPTURES USED IN THIS SECTION

"For the love of money is a root of all kinds of evil. Some people, eager for money, have wandered from the faith

and pierced themselves with many griefs."
—1 TIMOTHY 6:10

"I know what it is to be in need, and I know what it is to have plenty. I have learned the secret of being content in any and every situation, whether well fed or hungry, whether living in plenty or in want."
—PHILIPPIANS 4:12

"Do not be deceived: God cannot be mocked. A man reaps what he sows. Whoever sows to please their flesh, from the flesh will reap destruction; whoever sows to please the Spirit, from the Spirit will reap eternal life. Let us not become weary in doing good, for at the proper time we will reap a harvest if we do not give up."
—GALATIANS 6:7-9

A PRAYER ON MONEY

God, I'm looking to You to help me with my money
It can be tricky; it can be funny
But I know You're my provider and You have my back
And I can count on You; I know that's a fact
Into my finances I invite You in
I trust in You to show me where to begin
Lead me, guide me, and show me the way
Even in this area, I will do what You say
When I obey You, I am blessed through and through
I prosper with everything I put my hand to
So I don't lean on what I understand
Instead, I'm looking to You for the plan
I offer up my finances to You
You're the Lord of it all; show me what to do
I know it represents how I spend so much of my time
So I give You oversight over every dime
Lead me; guide me; in everything, I will do what You want me to
You are my compass, always right beside me. I'll do my budget
with You

SCRIPTURES USED IN THIS PRAYER

"Call to me and I will answer you and tell you great and unsearchable things you do not know." —JEREMIAH 33:3

"And my God will meet all your needs according to the riches of his glory in Christ Jesus" —PHILIPPIANS 4:19

"Commit to the LORD whatever you do, and he will establish your plans." —**PROVERBS 16:3**

"Show me the way I should go, for to you I entrust my life." —**PSALM 143:8B**

"Now it shall be, if you diligently obey the LORD your God, being careful to do all His commandments which I command you today, the Lord your God will set you high above all the nations of the earth. All these blessings will come upon you and overtake you if you obey the LORD your God." —**DEUTERONOMY 28:1-2, NASB1995**

"And let the favor of the Lord our God be upon us; and establish thou the work of our hands upon us; Yea, the work of our hands establish thou it." —**PSALM 90:17, ASV**

"Trust in the LORD with all your heart and lean not on your own understanding." —**PROVERBS 3:5**

"I lift up my eyes to the mountains— where does my help come from? My help comes from the LORD, the Maker of heaven and earth." —**PSALM 121:1-2**

"Teach me your way, LORD, that I may rely on your faithfulness; give me an undivided heart, that I may fear your name." —**PSALM 86:11**

"But when he, the Spirit of truth, comes, he will guide you into all the truth." —**JOHN 16:13A**

M

MONEY

PERSONALIZED SCRIPTURE DECLARATIONS ABOUT MONEY

2 CHRONICLES 1:11-12

God, help my heart's longing to be like the wise King Solomon, who did not ask for wealth, possessions, or honor. No! He didn't want the death of his enemies. The king didn't even request a longer life. But his desire was for wisdom and knowledge to help him to govern Your people. This is the cry of my heart, too, Lord; like You gave to Solomon, will You give me wisdom and knowledge, along with wealth, possessions, and honor?

PROVERBS 3:9

God, I honor You with my wealth. That is the first thing I do when I get my paycheck: I give to You, God.

PROVERBS 13:11

Dishonest money disappears, but when we gather and save money little by little, it grows. So that is what I choose to do! I honor You with my money.

ECCLESIASTES 5:10

I do not love money because I know that money will never bring fulfillment. You are my satisfaction, God!

MATTHEW 6:1-4

I do not flaunt my godly deeds in front of other people to be seen by them. I know that if I do, I will have no reward from my Father in heaven. When I give to the needy, I do not announce it with trumpets, as the hypocrites do, to be honored by people around me. Those people already have received their reward in full. But

M

MONEY

when I give to people who are in need, I don't let my left hand know what my right hand is doing so that my giving may be in secret. Then my Father, who sees what is done in secret, will reward me.

MATTHEW 6:24

I serve You, God, not money.

ROMANS 13:8

I don't owe anything to anyone but to love them. And what a relief that is! I do my part today in walking in love and being at peace with everybody as much as it's up to me on my end of things.

1 TIMOTHY 6:10

I do not love money because I know that the love of money is the root of all evil. Some people who are eager for money have wandered from the faith and received all sorts of consequences.

1 TIMOTHY 6:17-19

I choose not to be arrogant, and I don't put my hope in wealth, which is such an unstable thing to trust in, but I put my trust in You, God. You richly provide me with everything for my enjoyment. I do good. I am rich in good deeds and am generous and willing to share. In this way, I lay up treasure for myself as a firm foundation for the coming age so that I take hold of the life that is truly for me.

HEBREWS 13:5

I actively keep my life free from the love of money and am satisfied with what I have because, God, You have promised never to leave me or forsake me.

DEUTERONOMY 8:17-18

I do not say that my power and the strength of my hands produce wealth for me. But I will remember that it's You, God, who gives me the ability to produce wealth so that my life may confirm Your covenant.

DEUTERONOMY 15:10

I choose to give generously and without a grudge in my heart; because of this, You, Lord God, bless me in all my work, and everything I put my hand to will prosper.

1 CHRONICLES 29:9

Whenever I give, it is freely, easy-breezy, with no strings attached, and with all of my heart as unto You, Lord.

MALACHI 3:10-11

I bring the whole tithe into the storehouse so that there may be food in God's house. You told us to test You in this way, and You will "throw open the floodgates of heaven and pour out so much blessing that there will not be room enough to store it." You will prevent pests from devouring my crops, and the vines in my fields will not drop their fruit before it is ripe. Then You said that all the nations will call me blessed, for my land will be a delightful land.

MATTHEW 6:19-21

I do not store up for myself treasures on earth, where moths, bugs, and wild animals can destroy and where thieves break in and steal. But instead, I store up my riches in heaven, where nothing can access them but You! Where my treasure is, there my heart will be too, and my heart is with You!

M

MONEY

LUKE 6:38

When I give, it is given back to me. A good measure, pressed down, shaken together, and running over, it will be poured into my lap overflowing. It is with the measure I use that it will be measured to me. So it is that with the amount I give, it will be given back to me.

LUKE 16:10

Since I can be trusted with the very little things, I can also be trusted with the big things, and whoever is dishonest with very little will also be dishonest with much.

ACTS 20:35

It is a bigger blessing for me to give to someone than it is for me to receive.

2 CORINTHIANS 9:6-8

I know that if I sow small, I reap small, and if I sow without holding back, I reap over and above all I could ask or think! I give what I feel led in my spirit to give, not reluctantly or under any pressure, because, God, You love an *enthusiastic*, heartfelt giver, not someone who gives out of compulsion. You, of course, *can*, and I know You *want* to bless me abundantly so that in *all* things and at all times, I will abound in every good work.

2 CORINTHIANS 9:10

God, You supply seed for me to sow and bread for me to eat. You also make a way and increase my backup stash of seed and enlarge the harvest of my righteousness.

1 TIMOTHY 6:17-19

I am not prideful, and I don't put my hope in having a lot of money either, which comes and goes, but instead, I put my hope in You, God, who richly provides me with everything I need for my enjoyment! I do good, I am rich in good deeds, and I am generous and willing to share. In this way, I lay up treasure for myself as a firm foundation for the coming age so that I may take hold of the life that is truly the life You want me to live.

Chapter 14
NEVER HAVE I EVER

Being satisfied is rare. Most people seem to be miserable most of the time. When someone is genuinely content, it's exciting to see, contagious even. People are captivated and pull up a chair to watch someone who is truly happy. They demand and want to know *why* you are happy.

I know this because I have been both: satisfied and miserable. For me, the only thing that has brought deep fulfillment is to know God and to be known by Him. I don't mean this in a way as to say I am so special that I know Him. I know anyone can have a close relationship with Him. It's just walking closely with Him every day. I love that old song, "Just a Closer Walk With Thee":

Just a closer walk with thee

Grant it, Jesus, is my plea

(I thought it was "if you please" forever, and I still accidentally say that sometimes—ha ha.)

I'll be satisfied as long

As I walk, let me walk close to Thee.

I have a different walk with God than I have ever had before. It is unlike any other relationship. But what is similar to other relational dynamics is that it keeps growing according to what we put into it. I am so thankful to Him. The more steps I take with God, the more I am captured by Him. I have seen so many people transformed by Him: sinners turned into some of the most passionate people I know, living purely for Jesus.

The devotion someone has to God is personal but also can be so contagious. I have seen it over and over again in my life. Never have I ever seen a book like the Bible where I could read the same thing, and it has such a different meaning. Or when I speak a message that I believe God has had me preach, I often will have the people in the room tell me about what they have gotten from what I said, and they have all gotten different things. That is so cool. There is always more of God. Never have I ever been more convinced, more satisfied, and more content than with God. Everyone is invited to His party. It's up to you to attend.

A PRAYER ON PUTTING GOD FIRST

Never have I ever been satisfied by something more than You
Even though, like everyone else, I've tried to be with a thing or two
But I always come running back straight into Your arms
You're the one who wreaks havoc on all the world's charms
Because in You my needs are supplied
I don't wander, looking left and right
I look straight into Your eyes
I'm so grateful for the peace that You supply
You're the one that I want as I search the world up and down
The missing puzzle piece for my soul, You're my hope that I found
No one else can meet my needs the way You do
You're the one who set the stars; You always see me through
You're mysterious and fascinating
Interesting and captivating
It's unending the things I discover about You
When I don't get distracted, I know just what to do
Your facets are like the sides of a diamond
Just when I learn one thing about You, You become new to me again
Forever You are faithful
Your mercies never come to an end
I am never bored when I am seeking Your face
It's when I look away that I get displaced
But when I look to You, I remember who I am
Everything makes sense and I am calm again
You lead me by still waters and You restore my soul
When I am in Your presence, You are in control

I am trusting in You, God; You are my heart's desire

And if I veer to the right or left, I get back with You; You restart my fire

You restore to me the joy of my salvation

You help me when I am in a heart evaluation

I want to grow and do what You've called me to

God, never have I ever found someone like You

SCRIPTURES USED IN THIS PRAYER

"And earth has nothing I desire besides You." **—PSALM 73:25B**

"And my God will meet all your needs according to the riches of his glory in Christ Jesus." **—PHILIPPIANS 4:19**

"But my eyes are fixed on You, Sovereign LORD."
—PSALM 141:8A

"God set these lights in the sky to light the earth."
—GENESIS 1:17, NLT

"You will keep in perfect peace those whose minds are steadfast, because they trust in You." **—ISAIAH 26:3**

"He makes me lie down in green pastures, he leads me beside quiet waters, he refreshes my soul. He guides me along the right paths for his name's sake." **—PSALM 23:2-3**

"Restore to me the joy of Your salvation and grant me a willing spirit, to sustain me." **—PSALM 51:12**

PERSONALIZED SCRIPTURE DECLARATIONS TO HELP PUT GOD FIRST

PSALM 16:11

God, You make Your path of life known to me; You fill me with joy in Your presence, with eternal pleasures at Your right hand.

PSALM 17:15

As for me, You are my vindicator, and I see Your face; when I wake up, I will be satisfied when I see You.

PSALM 37:4

You bring joy to me, Lord, and You give me the desires of my heart.

PSALM 63:2-3

I have seen You in the sanctuary, and I saw Your power and Your glory. Because Your love is better than life, everything I say will bring glory to You.

PSALM 90:14

Lord, You satisfy me in the morning with Your unfailing love, so I sing for joy and am happy all of my days.

PSALM 91:16

With long life, You satisfy me and show me Your salvation.

PSALM 107:9

You satisfy my thirsty heart and fill the hungry with good things.

PROVERBS 19:23

I respect You, Lord; it leads to life! I choose to rest content, untouched by trouble.

ISAIAH 58:11

Lord, You guide me always; You satisfy my needs, even in the emptiest and most worn-out times of my life, and You strengthen my very frame. I will be like a well-watered garden, like a spring whose waters never fail.

JEREMIAH 31:25

You refresh me when I am exhausted, and You are my satisfaction when I feel like giving up.

MATTHEW 5:6

I hunger and thirst to be at right standing with You, God, and I am filled.

MATTHEW 6:33

I seek first Your kingdom, God, and Your righteousness, and all these things are given to me as well.

JOHN 14:6

Jesus, You are the way, the truth, and the life. No one comes to the Father except through You!

ACTS 4:12

Salvation is found in no one but Jesus; there is no other name under heaven by which I can be saved.

ROMANS 15:13

The God of hope fills me with all joy and peace as I trust

in Him, and I overflow with hope by the power of the Holy Spirit.

PHILIPPIANS 4:11-13

I have learned to be content, whatever the circumstances. I know what it is to be in need, and I know what it is to have plenty. I have learned the secret of being content in any and every situation, whether well-fed or hungry, whether living in plenty or want. I can do all things through You, who gives me strength.

PHILIPPIANS 4:19

And I know that You, God, will meet all my needs according to the riches of Your glory in Jesus.

1 TIMOTHY 6:6

I have godliness with contentment, and it is of significant gain to me.

HEBREWS 13:5

I keep my life free from the love of money and am content with what I have, God, because You said, "Never will I leave you; never will I forsake you."

Chapter 15
OFFERING

God, You are my life's greatest gift. No one, nothing, satisfies like You do. There is simply no one like You. My life is my offering.

I have seen a lot of people walk with Jesus. Some grow quickly with Him as they give their lives completely as an offering in absolute surrender. Some people just ask God into their lives but sort of stop there at the introduction of the relationship. Some grow bored and have a mixed life with the world and don't even realize it's contaminated. I have started to discover the meaning of losing your life to find it. I love Him. When you really dive in and decide to do what it takes to live whatever way He is calling you to, it is amazing. Satisfaction is found in offering our lives in obedience to Him.

A life yielded to Him is so sweet. I just have today to give. Not yesterday or tomorrow. So how can I do my best today? Right now? My life is my offering. Anything less just wouldn't be enough. I love You with all my heart, God; the closer I get to You, the more I love You, and the more I want to surrender. We find our lives when we lose them. I give it all over and over.

SCRIPTURES USED IN THIS SECTION

"But I will rejoice even if I lose my life, pouring it out like a liquid offering to God, just like your faithful service is an offering to God. And I want all of you to share that joy."
—PHILIPPIANS 2:17, NLT

"I will freely sacrifice to You; I will praise Your name, O Lord, for it is good."
—PSALM 54:6A, NKJV

"Whoever finds their life will lose it, and whoever loses their life for my sake will find it."
—MATTHEW 10:39

O

OFFERING

A PRAYER ON OFFERING

My life is my offering, my love letter to You
I've been wondering today what You have for me to do
I will not lean on what I understand
I trust in You, God; I comply with Your plan
Masterful is Your brushstroke and so close is Your aid for me
I marvel at Your creation; every day, You have something new to see
I am studying You closely because I know You hold the key
My life is Your workmanship
I am not here to do my own thing
I refuse to live in complacency, just on the hamster wheel of boredom
I wake up every morning *excited* and not numb
I'm activated and resolute—I run toward what You're saying
All of my days are in Your hands; that is what I'm praying
There is a trap: if I do everything right, I can *earn* Your love
But that is not true; I was bought with Your blood
We are all equal in Your eyes and I know this is true
That I can't lose or earn more, so it is by choice I stay with You
I offer myself completely, 100 percent, to You
There is no one else between us—what You say, I do

SCRIPTURES USED IN THIS PRAYER

"In you, Lord my God, I put my trust." —PSALM 25:1

"We do not know what to do, but our eyes are on you."
—2 CHRONICLES 20:12B

"Trust in the LORD with all your heart and lean not on your own understanding." —**PROVERBS 3:5**

"But blessed is the one who trusts in the LORD, whose con-fidence is in him." —**JEREMIAH 17:7**

"But as for me, the nearness of God is my good; I have made the Lord GOD my refuge, That I may tell of all Your works." —**PSALM 73:28, NASB1995**

"Great is his faithfulness; his mercies begin afresh each morning." —**LAMENTATIONS 3:23, NLT**

"For we are God's handiwork, created in Christ Jesus to do good works, which God prepared in advance for us to do." —**EPHESIANS 2:10**

"Yet not my will, but yours be done." —**LUKE 22:42B**

"Because I am righteous, I will see you. When I awake, I will see you face to face and be satisfied." —**PSALM 17:15, NLT**

"My times are in your hands; deliver me from the hands of my enemies, from those who pursue me." —**PSALM 31:15**

"For you know that it was not with perishable things such as silver or gold that you were redeemed from the empty way of life handed down to you from your ancestors, but with the precious blood of Christ, a lamb without blemish or defect." —**1 PETER 1:18-19**

"For God does not show favoritism." —**ROMANS 2:11**

PERSONALIZED SCRIPTURE DECLARATIONS TO OFFER YOUR LIFE TO GOD

HEBREWS 13:15-16

Through You, Jesus, I continually offer to God a sacrifice of praise—the fruit of my lips that proudly speaks Your name. And I do not forget to do good and to share with others; with these sacrifices, God, I know You are pleased.

EPHESIANS 2:10

I am Your handiwork, God, created in Christ Jesus to do good works, which You prepared ahead of time for me to do.

MATTHEW 10:39

Whoever finds their life will lose it, and whoever loses their life for Your sake, Jesus, will find it.

MATTHEW 16:24

Jesus, You told Your disciples that whoever wants to be a follower of Yours must refuse themselves and take up their cross and follow You. I do that with Your help with all my heart every day with every choice I make.

EPHESIANS 5:1-2

God, I choose to follow Your example and walk in the way of LOVE, just as Jesus loved me so much that He gave Himself as a fragrant offering and sacrifice to God.

O

OFFERING

1 CORINTHIANS 6:19-20

My body is the temple of the Holy Spirit, who lives in me, and was given to me by You, God. I am not my own; I was bought at a price. So I choose to honor You, God, with my body.

ROMANS 12:1

In light of Your mercy, God, I give my body as a living sacrifice, holy and pleasing to You—this is my true and proper worship.

ROMANS 6:19

Just as I used to live a life of impurity and I only grew in wickedness, now I am the opposite! I am entirely committed to righteousness which I know leads to holiness.

PROVERBS 23:26

I give You my heart, God, and I let my eyes delight in Your ways.

ISAIAH 6:8

Then I heard the voice of the Lord saying, "Whom shall I send? And who will go for us?" And I answered, "Here am I. Send me!"

JAMES 4:7

I surrender myself to You, God. I resist the devil, and he will flee from me!

O

Chapter 16
PRAYER

Prayer is talking to God. It is so vital that your communication lines stay open. They are so important. Like any relationship, talking is the life flow, the wellspring of blood to the heart of the connection. When it stops, so too does the source of connectivity.

I have shifted this last season after some major trials to being in a new place, more like Mary than Martha; if you know this story, you know it's a good shift. Jesus was coming to see Martha and Mary, but then Martha ran and got busy preparing a meal for Him (imagine *that* hostess anxiety: Jesus came to her house), and Mary sat and listened to Him. Mary complained, "Jesus, make her help me!" I believe most of us can relate to this moment, ha ha. She was so bold to even say this to Jesus, but they were friends, I think. I don't know that for sure. She spoke to Jesus as a friend. He explained, "Martha, you run around with all these preparations, but Mary is doing the right thing by sitting with Me."

This is convicting to me. I feel so grateful to God for all He has done in and through me, and to get to talk to Him is an honor. What I have learned is to talk to Him more. It's like the voice of a friend; you get more closely acquainted with

Him the more time you spend with Him. The more time you spend with Him, the more you understand Him. I love praying, "Where else would I go? You have the words of eternal life." I quote this to Him frequently from my heart, saying, "God, when everything else feels unsteady, You are who I run to! You are my solid rock!"

Just like everyone else, I have had questions. Guess what? God can handle you and your questions! Even the pain you've endured. Bring it all to Him and talk it out. Work through it with Him. He was there through the things you've overcome. He knows what is going on. Don't grow tired when you're waiting on Him. He is always right on time. I know our relationships are all different because we are all different, but He is not. He is the same yesterday, today, and forever.

I trust Him. You can trust Him. He loves us. The more I talk to Him, the more I realize He likes to be included in our lives. I also have learned that instead of just guessing what He means by things, I ask Him. It's a friendship.

SCRIPTURES USED IN THIS SECTION

"As Jesus and his disciples were on their way, he came to a village where a woman named Martha opened her home to him. She had a sister called Mary, who sat at the Lord's feet listening to what he said. But Martha was distracted by all the preparations that had to be made. She came to him and asked, 'Lord, don't you care that my sister has left me to do the work by myself? Tell her to help me!' 'Martha, Martha,' the Lord answered, 'you are worried and upset about many things, but few things are needed—or indeed only one. Mary has chosen what is better, and it will not be taken away from her.'"
—**LUKE 10:38-42**

"Simon Peter answered him, 'Lord, to whom shall we go? You have the words of eternal life.'"

—JOHN 6:68

"The Lord is my rock, my fortress and my deliverer; my God is my rock, in whom I take refuge, my shield and the horn of my salvation, my stronghold."

—PSALM 18:2

"Jesus Christ is the same yesterday and today and forever."

—HEBREWS 13:8

A PRAYER ON PRIORITIZING PRAYER

God, prayer is so cool—it's just talking to You!
I do it all day long and it's all I want to do
So I go about my day and let You in on everything
I love sharing life with You and all the joy it brings
Talking to You like a friend has brought me peace
It relieves me and soothes my suffering
I spend time with You in the morning and all day long
And when I hear the birds, I know You're the reason for their song
I come to You honestly and tell You how I feel
You know it all anyway, so why not be real
You love me as I am; You love me all day through
There is nothing You don't care about, so I bring it all to You
I don't know how You do it – omnipresent everywhere
When other people are mad at You, I know that You *still* care
I tell them to run right to You, to tell You everything
That You're right there with them and *honest* answers You will bring
You can be trusted because You are true
When I need to work through something, I bring it straight to You
You can handle all my questions; You can handle any fear
So I come boldly to Your throne of grace because I belong right there
You are faithful in the morning, faithful through the pain
Faithful through the highs and lows, You remain the same
I pray and ask You how You feel because You are so real
You can be trusted every day with how I feel

SCRIPTURES USED IN THIS PRAYER

"One thing I ask from the LORD, this only do I seek: that I may dwell in the house of the LORD all the days of my life, to gaze on the beauty of the LORD and to seek him in his temple." **—PSALM 27:4**

"Don't worry about anything; instead, pray about every-thing. Tell God what you need, and thank him for all he has done." **—PHILIPPIANS 4:6, NLT**

"There I will go to the altar of God, to God—the source of all my joy." **—PSALM 43:4A, NLT**

"Now may the Lord of peace himself give you peace at all times in every way. The Lord be with you all." **—2 THESSALO-NIANS 3:16, ESV**

"And the peace of God, which transcends all understand-ing, will guard your hearts and your minds in Christ Jesus." **—PHILIPPIANS 4:7**

"Evening and morning and at noon I will pray, and cry aloud, And He shall hear my voice." **—PSALM 55:17, NKJV**

"Trust in him at all times, you people; pour out your hearts to him, for God is our refuge." **—PSALM 62:8**

"The Lord appeared to us in the past, saying: 'I have loved you with an everlasting love; I have drawn you with unfail-ing kindness.'" **—JEREMIAH 31:3**

"Where can I go from your Spirit? Where can I flee from your presence? If I go up to the heavens, you are there; if I make my bed in the depths, you are there. If I rise on the wings of the dawn, if I settle on the far side of the sea, even there your hand will guide me, your right hand will hold me fast." **—PSALM 139:7-10**

"Behold, You desire truth in the innermost being, and in the hidden part You will make me know wisdom." —**PSALM 51:6, NASB1995**

"God's way is perfect. All the LORD's promises prove true. He is a shield for all who look to him for protection." —**PSALM 18:30, NLT**

"Call to me and I will answer you, and will tell you great and hidden things that you have not known." —**JEREMIAH 33:3, ESV**

"So let us come boldly to the throne of our gracious God. There we will receive his mercy, and we will find grace to help us when we need it most." —**HEBREWS 4:16, NLT**

"If we are unfaithful, he remains faithful, for he cannot deny who he is." —**2 TIMOTHY 2:13, NLT**

"God is not human, that he should lie, not a human being, that he should change his mind. Does he speak and then not act? Does he promise and not fulfill?" —**NUMBERS 23:19**

PERSONALIZED SCRIPTURE DECLARATIONS TO NAVIGATE YOUR PRAYER LIFE

1 CHRONICLES 16:11

I look to You, God, and Your strength; I seek Your face always. As I draw near to You, You draw near to me!

2 CHRONICLES 6:21

Father, thank You that You hear my cries and the longing of my heart when I pray and talk to You. You tune in to me from heaven, and when You hear, You forgive.

2 CHRONICLES 7:14

God, You inspired me when You challenged Your people by exclaiming, "If my people, who are called by my name, will humble themselves and pray and seek my face and turn from their wicked ways, then I will hear from heaven and I will forgive their sin and will heal their land." So I humble myself, pray, seek You, and repent for any wrongdoing. I receive Your forgiveness and healing for our land.

JEREMIAH 29:11-13

Thank You, God, that Your plans cause me to prosper and do not put me in danger; Your plans give me hope and a bright future. When I call on You and pray to You, You listen to me. I seek You and I find You because I seek You with all of my heart.

JOB 22:27

When I pray, God, You hear me and fulfill my requests. You are the God of the follow-through!

PSALM 4:1

Please answer me when I call to You, God. Give me relief from my torment; have mercy on me and hear the requests of my heart.

PSALM 17:6

I call on You, my God. You always answer me; You turn Your ear to me and hear my prayer!

PSALM 141:2

God, I want my prayer to be set before You like the best-smelling perfume; when I lift my hands up to You, may it be a true sacrifice to You.

PSALM 145:18-19

Lord, You are near to me when I call on You; in fact, I know You are close to all the people who call on You in truth and honesty. You satisfy my desires and the cry of all who fear You; You hear what we say and save us.

PROVERBS 15:8

Father, I know that You cannot stand the sacrifice of the wicked, but the prayer of the upright pleases You.

PROVERBS 15:29

God, You told us You are far from the wicked, but You hear the prayer of the righteous.

MATTHEW 5:44

I know You want me to love my enemies and to pray for those who persecute me and speak negatively about me, so I choose to do that right now; enable me to do that with Your strength.

MATTHEW 7:11

If evil people who aren't even serving You know how to give good gifts to their children, how much more will *You*, my Father in heaven, give good gifts to me when I ask You?!

MATTHEW 26:41

I watch, pray, and am mindful so that I will not fall into sin traps. The spirit is willing, but the flesh is weak. Help me to take the way of escape that You have provided for me in every temptation.

MARK 11:24

Whatever I ask for in prayer, I believe I have received it, and it is mine. Have Your way, God! I agree with You, on earth as it is in heaven!

LUKE 18:1

Just like You taught Your disciples, Jesus, I also always pray, and I don't give up. I haven't yet, and I never will, by Your grace!

ROMANS 8:26

The Spirit helps me in my weakness. When I do not know what I should pray for, the Holy Spirit Himself intercedes for me through sounds that have no words.

ROMANS 12:2

I do not become like the pattern of this world, but I am transformed by the renewing of my mind by meditating on the Bible. Then I can test and approve what Your will is, God, Your good, pleasing, and perfect will.

ROMANS 12:12

I am joyful in hope, patient in suffering, and I keep showing up to talk to You in prayer.

EPHESIANS 1:18-19

I pray that the eyes of my heart may be enlightened so that I may know the hope that You have called me to, the riches of all You have stored up in Your holy people, and Your incomparably great power for us who believe.

EPHESIANS 6:18

And I pray in the spirit all the time, no matter what I am doing, with all kinds of prayers and requests. With this in mind, I am alert and aware, and I always keep on praying for Your people, Lord.

COLOSSIANS 4:2

I devote myself to prayer, being watchful and thankful.

1 THESSALONIANS 5:16-18

I celebrate always, pray consistently and give thanks no matter what is going on because this is the plan You have for me, God; this is Your will for me in Jesus. Give me Your prayer strategy. What is on Your heart, God?

1 TIMOTHY 2:1-2

I cry out to You, God, on behalf of other people. I talk to You honestly. I stand in the gap between You and other people in intercession and thanksgiving for everybody—for kings and all those in authority—so that I may live a peaceful and quiet life in all godliness and holiness.

1 TIMOTHY 2:8

When I pray, I lift up holy hands without anger or revenge. I get my heart right, humble myself, and stay and live in peace with other people as much as it's up to me!

JAMES 1:5-6

When I lack wisdom, I ask You, God; You give generously to everybody without finding fault, and You give to me freely. But when I ask, I must believe and not doubt because the one who doubts is like a wave of the sea, blown and tossed by the wind.

JAMES 5:13

When I am in trouble, I talk to You, God. When I am happy, I sing songs of praise and honor to exalt You above all else!

JAMES 5:16

I confess my sins to someone I trust and pray for other people so that I may be healed. Because I am a righteous person who is in right standing with You, my prayer is powerful and impactful.

1 JOHN 1:9

When I tell someone (confess and admit) what I have done, God, You are faithful, just, and will forgive me of my sins and purify me from all unrighteousness.

1 JOHN 5:14-15

This is the confidence I have in approaching You, God: that if I ask anything according to Your will, *You hear me*.

PRAYER

Since I know You hear me—no matter what I ask—I know that I have what I ask You for, as long as it is in line with Your will and Your Word!

Chapter 17
QUITTING

I refuse to quit changing. I refuse to quit obeying God's will. I refuse to quit following the path of God's plan for my life. I refuse to stop holding on to hope for my life. Without Him, where would we be? Quitting life isn't an option. I choose not to quit growing, advancing, and gaining more understanding of who God is and how I can be closer to Him. I will never leave the pursuit to become the person He has called me to be—not what I think I should be or what other people expect me to be. Because who are we kidding?! We can't please people if we try!

But to be what God has created me to be, to please You, God—that is my heart's desire. So to do that, I give You my heart. I give You my attention, my affection. I give You my admiration.

I have noticed that what we focus on grows. So I quit focusing on the wrong things. I stop focusing on myself so much. I stop focusing on the bad reports. I start focusing on You—on Your still, small voice. I trust You, God. You are so worthy of praise and focus. I love You. I trust You. You grow in my heart. I focus my heart on You. I quit worrying.

It's so easy to quit our New Year's resolutions, to quit the things that are good for us. What if we quit the things that are bad for us? Let's get into healthy habits together! Let's fight for the good; why not? Our lives are only as good as our days are.

SCRIPTURES USED IN THIS SECTION

"So we make it our goal to please him."
—2 CORINTHIANS 5:9A

"And after the earthquake a fire, but the Lord was not in the fire; and after the fire a still small voice."
—1 KINGS 19:12, NKJV

A PRAYER ON QUITTING

I quit worry and strife and fearing and dread
I quit all the antagonizing things in my head
I refuse to quit on what matters most
I stay in the lane of activation and hope
I'm always willing to change the areas that need to grow
I won't settle in knowing just what I know
I am God's work of art that is always improving
And I'm not staying here; I'm going to keep on moving
I am mesmerized by the truth; I am committed to learning
I am willing to do what it takes to keep burning
Burning for life, burning with desire
I refuse to quit living with fire
So many people let the door hit them in the rear
Going through life with no senses to adhere
I've been there before; I didn't know if I'd wake up
This is how people become zombies and mouth-breathers
and stuff
There have been these moments when life has been real rough
In those times, I realized why people didn't want to wake up
Sometimes feeling your feelings makes you feel like you've
had enough
But man, I would much rather be alive
To have air in my lungs than just try to survive
Every feeling there is, that's what I want to feel
The whole hero's journey is life, and it is real
I would rather be alive and going through the cycle of growth
Than hiding in my circumstances so I can die alone
It's not comforting to be stagnant; it's not okay to stay the same
I have learned I have to choose my pain

And it's the pain it takes to not remain
I want to get out of my cocoon
I don't want to stay in the same room
And I'm pumping my wings inside this dark space
It sometimes hurts to grow, but it's worse to remain the same
So I will do whatever it takes to quit what entangles me
The obstacles that hold me back can no longer be
So I quit worrying, fear, and dread
And all of the antagonizing things in my head

SCRIPTURES USED IN THIS PRAYER

"I sought the LORD, and he answered me; he delivered me from all my fears." **—PSALM 34:4**

"Yet this I call to mind and therefore I have hope: Because of the LORD's great love we are not consumed, for his compassions never fail. They are new every morning; great is your faithfulness." **—LAMENTATIONS 3:21-23**

"But we all, with unveiled face, beholding as in a mirror the glory of the Lord, are being transformed into the same image from glory to glory, just as by the Spirit of the Lord." **—2 CORINTHIANS 3:18, NKJV**

"For we are God's handiwork, created in Christ Jesus to do good works, which God prepared in advance for us to do." **—EPHESIANS 2:10**

"They will still bear fruit in old age, they will stay fresh and green." **—PSALM 92:14**

"If you are willing and obedient, you will eat the good things of the land." **—ISAIAH 1:19**

"But if I say, 'I will not mention his word or speak anymore in his name,' his word is in my heart like a fire, a fire shut up in my bones. I am weary of holding it in; indeed, I cannot."
—JEREMIAH 20:9

"Enter through the narrow gate. For wide is the gate and broad is the road that leads to destruction, and many enter through it." **—MATTHEW 7:13**

"This is why it is said: 'Wake up, sleeper, rise from the dead, and Christ will shine on you.'" **—EPHESIANS 5:14**

"But I discipline my body and make it my slave, so that, after I have preached to others, I myself will not be disqualified."
—1 CORINTHIANS 9:27, NASB1995

"Therefore, since we are surrounded by such a great cloud of witnesses, let us throw off everything that hinders and the sin that so easily entangles. And let us run with perseverance the race marked out for us." **—HEBREWS 12:1**

PERSONALIZED SCRIPTURE DECLARATIONS TO HELP YOU REFUSE TO QUIT

1 CHRONICLES 16:10-11

I give glory to Your holy name, God, when I seek You, and my heart rejoices. I look to You, Lord, and Your strength. I look for Your face always. I won't stop seeking You!

2 CHRONICLES 15:7

But as for me, I am strong and do not give up; I am confident my work will be majorly rewarded!

PSALM 16:8

I keep my eyes always on You, God. With You right by my side, I will not be shaken! I cannot be moved! I choose to stick close to You!

PSALM 27:13-14

I remain confident of this: I will see Your goodness, Father, in my lifetime. I wait for You, Lord. I am strong, and I am full of courage, and I boldly wait for You.

PSALM 37:23-24

You make my steps firm as I find my joy in You. Even if I stumble, I will not fall. You uphold me with Your hand.

PSALM 55:22

I cast my cares on You, God, and You sustain me! I am so thankful that You will never let Your righteous people be unsteady!

MATTHEW 19:26

> With human strength, it is impossible, but with You, God, all things are possible!

ACTS 20:24

> I consider my life worth nothing to me; my only aim is to finish the race that You have set before me and complete the task You have given me—the assignment of testifying to the good news of Your grace, God.

ROMANS 5:3-5

> I remember there is good in the things I go through because I know that when I go through things, they produce perseverance; perseverance produces character; character produces hope. And hope does not disappoint me because Your love, God, has been poured out into my heart through the Holy Spirit, who has been given to me freely.

ROMANS 12:12

> I am joyful in hope, patient in affliction, and faithful in prayer.

ROMANS 12:21

> I refuse to be overcome by evil; instead, I overcome evil with good!

1 CORINTHIANS 9:24

> In a race, all the runners run, but only one gets to win the first-place prize. I choose to run in a way, so I finish in that first-place spot; I run with the end in mind. I run and do not grow weary. I run at a steady pace and in a way to win!

1 CORINTHIANS 10:13

The temptations I face are not news to You, God. You are faithful; You will not let me be tempted beyond what I can bear. But when I am tempted, You will also provide a way out so that I can endure it. I choose to take the way of escape You've created for me!

1 CORINTHIANS 16:13

I am on my guard. I stand firm in the faith. I am bold, very courageous, and extremely strong only because my strength is in You, God.

2 CORINTHIANS 4:8-9

I may be squeezed in on every side, but at least I am not completely crushed; perplexed, yes, but the good news is that I am not in despair or willing to give up. I may be persecuted, but I have not been left abandoned; struck down, but not destroyed in the middle of the battles I have been facing. So really, that is a lot of good news. I choose to focus on good things!

2 CORINTHIANS 12:9

God, Your grace is enough for me. Your power is made perfect in my weakness. I boast gladly about my weaknesses so that Jesus' power may rest on me.

GALATIANS 6:9

I do not become tired in doing good because, at the right time, I will reap a harvest if I do not give up. Giving up is not even an option for me! I refuse to consider it.

PHILIPPIANS 1:6

I am confident of this, that You who started the good

work in me will carry it on to complete fulfillment until the day Jesus comes back.

PHILIPPIANS 3:14

I press on toward the goal to win the prize that You, God, have called me to in Jesus.

PHILIPPIANS 4:13

I can do all this through You, Jesus, who gives me strength.

COLOSSIANS 3:23-24

In whatever I do, I work at it with all my heart, like I am working for You, Lord, not for human leaders, since I know that I will get an inheritance from You as a reward. It is You who I am serving. So I do my work as if I am doing it directly for You!

2 TIMOTHY 4:7

I have fought the good fight. I have finished the race. I have kept the faith!

HEBREWS 12:1-3

Because I am surrounded by such a great cloud of witnesses, intentionally I throw things off that try to hinder me and slow me down, including the sin that can easily entangle me. I run with a pace of perseverance the race that You, God, marked out for me, locking my eyes on You, Jesus, the pioneer who went before me, blazing the trail and making the way. You are the one who makes my faith perfect. Because of the joy set before You, You endured the cross. I know You hated the shame that You suffered; then You sat down at the right hand of the throne of Your father, God. You did it all for me!

HEBREWS 12:11

There is nothing fun about discipline at the time; instead, it's painful! But it is worth it because it creates a harvest of righteous fruit and peace for those of us who have been trained by it.

HEBREWS 13:6

I speak out with confident peace, "The Lord is my helper; I refuse to be afraid. What can ordinary human beings do to me?"

JAMES 1:2-4

I consider it pure joy whenever I go through hard seasons because I am confident that the testing of my faith produces perseverance. I allow perseverance to finish its work so that I may be mature and complete, not lacking anything.

JAMES 1:12

Things always work out in my favor when I continue forward and pursue You, God, even when I am under trial, because when I keep enduring even through the tests, I will receive the crown of life that You have promised, Lord, to those who love You. I do love You with all my heart, and I will never quit.

Chapter 18
RELATIONSHIPS

God, I have heard life is like a book; some people are for pages, some are for chapters, and some are for the entire book. Some skip around in the pages of our lives. I say You are the author of my story, and You determine who is on my pages and when. I only want to be with the people You want me to be with, doing what You want me to do, going where You see me and when You see me there. My life is in Your hands. My days are Yours, not my own. The best days I have are when I walk them out according to what You have for me and not of my own doing—that I know for sure!

There are reasons for seasons of relationships. I have walked with people for seasons, and I am so thankful for them. They have helped me become who I am today, and hopefully, I have contributed to who they are as well.

I live by this excellent visual: there are levels of intimacy in our lives. Certain people belong in specific circles, starting with God and us in the innermost circle, then our mate if we get married, then our kids, then our friends, then acquaintances, then everyone else.

THE CIRCLE OF RELATIONSHIPS

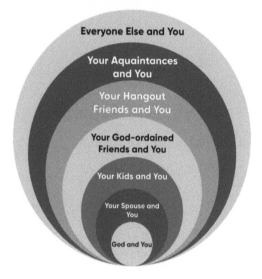

- · God and you
- · Your spouse and you
- · Your kids and you
- · Your nontoxic, life-giving, mutually beneficial, God-ordained friends and you
- · Your lighter, more surface hangout friends and you
- · Your acquaintances and you
- · Everyone else and you

It's so interesting how complicated this area of life can be, but it's simple at the same time. When things are in the right place, it is amazing how fulfilling relationships are when they aren't dysfunctional. And if they *are* dysfunctional, I know You know what to do, God. You know how to help me navigate and get me from here to there. You know how to untie every knot. Thank You for helping me get things to a healthy place inside myself and in my relationships.

We are human, so we are all a work in progress, but we are growing if we commit to that! A relationship can bring so

R

RELATIONSHIPS

much joy and so much pain at the same time. But when we are willing and committed to advance and develop, it is richly rewarding to be in a relationship that inspires and nourishes personal advancement

A PRAYER ON RELATIONSHIPS

God, in my relationships, I don't want to be just surviving

I invite You into each one so I can be thriving

I am open to Your every instruction

I want an immediate strife reduction

Advancement in peace

Advancement in love

I believe the increase comes from above

I am thankful for You, and I'm excited about the change

Show me my part and what to rearrange

I pray other people see me the way You do

I'll change my behavior; I'll work with You

For the advancement of Your kingdom, I humble myself

I want my relationships to be unlike anyone else

But I want to live what You have in mind

Not just the ordinary; I like the divine

A home run for You is a home run for me

I want what You want, so, God, please help me

SCRIPTURES USED IN THIS PRAYER

*"I will instruct you and teach you in the way you should go;
I will counsel you with my loving eye on you."* **—PSALM 32:8**

*"It is to one's honor to avoid strife, but every fool is quick to
quarrel."* **—PROVERBS 20:3**

*"And this is my prayer: that your love may abound more and
more in knowledge and depth of insight."* **—PHILIPPIANS 1:9**

R

RELATIONSHIPS

"Praise the LORD! Oh give thanks to the LORD, for he is good, for his steadfast love endures forever!" **—PSALM 106:1, ESV**

"The LORD make his face to shine upon you and be gracious to you; the LORD lift up his countenance upon you and give you peace." **—NUMBERS 6:25-26, ESV**

"For we are co-workers in God's service." **—1 CORINTHIANS 3:9A**

"Humble yourselves, therefore, under God's mighty hand, that he may lift you up in due time." **—1 PETER 5:6**

"However, as it is written: 'What no eye has seen, what no ear has heard and what no human mind has conceived'— the things God has prepared for those who love him— these are the things God has revealed to us by his Spir- it. The Spirit searches all things, even the deep things of God." **—1 CORINTHIANS 2:9-10**

"But my life is worth nothing to me unless I use it for finish- ing the work assigned me by the Lord Jesus—the work of telling others the Good News about the wonderful grace of God." **—ACTS 20:24, NLT**

PERSONALIZED SCRIPTURE DECLARATIONS TO ASSIST YOU IN YOUR RELATIONSHIPS

GENESIS 2:18

God, You have made it clear: "It is not good for the man to be alone. I will make a helper suitable for him." Thank You, God, for making a suitable helper for me, and in the meantime, I am fully satisfied in my season!

EPHESIANS 4:2-3

I am endeavoring to be 100 percent humble and gentle. I am patient. I am patient with other people and love without manipulative strings attached. I make every single effort to stay in unity and to keep the Spirit through the bond of peace.

PROVERBS 18:24

I choose reliable friends because I know the Bible says that a person who has friends who they can't count on quickly comes to ruin, but there is a friend who sticks closer than a brother. That is You, Jesus! I am asking for the right friends in this season of my life! Everyone in the proximity that You see because You have a different point of view than I do!

JOHN 13:34

I love other people the way You have loved me, God.

LUKE 14:28

I count the cost before I start new projects and endeavors, and I refuse to get distracted with my own or other people's lesser things that pull me away from my primary God-appointed assignments.

JOHN 13:35

By this, everyone will know that I am Your disciple: if I love other people.

JOHN 15:13

There is no greater love than to lay down my life for my friends.

ROMANS 12:10

I am devoted to other people in love. I honor others above myself.

ROMANS 14:19

I make every effort to do what leads to peace and mutual edification.

1 CORINTHIANS 13:6-7

Your love in me, God, does not delight in evil but rejoices with the truth. It always protects, trusts, hopes, and perseveres.

1 CORINTHIANS 16:14

Everything I do is done in love.

2 CORINTHIANS 6:13

God, help me to navigate the dynamics of my relationships with You and other people. I will not be in an unhealthy situation or work together and too tightly yoke myself with people who are not living for You, Jesus. What do righteousness and wickedness have in common? Or what companionship can light have with darkness? So show me Your heart here, God, and how I can keep it in proper balance—having a heart for people but not being too closely intertwined with people who aren't making You their priority.

EPHESIANS 4:32

I am kind and compassionate to others, and I quickly forgive other people with ease, just like You, God, forgave me.

PHILIPPIANS 2:3-4

I don't do anything to pursue my own way or in my own strength. Rather, in humility, I value others above myself, not looking to my interests but to the interests of others.

PHILIPPIANS 2:5-7

In my relationships, I choose to have the same mindset as You, Jesus. Even though You are in very nature God, You did not consider Your equality with God as something to be used to Your advantage; instead, You made Yourself nothing by taking the very nature of a servant, being made in human likeness.

COLOSSIANS 3:13-14

I am patient with other people and forgive them, even when upsetting things come up. I forgive as You, Lord, forgave me. And over all these virtues, I put on love, which binds us all together in perfect unity.

1 THESSALONIANS 5:11

I encourage other people and work to build them up.

HEBREWS 10:24-25

I think about how I may motivate other people into love and doing good things, not stopping getting together in

RELATIONSHIPS

unity for Jesus, as some are in the habit of doing, but encouraging other people—and all the more as I see the day that Jesus comes back approaching.

JAMES 1:19-20

I listen first, I am slow to speak, and I rarely become angry because human anger does not produce the righteousness that God desires.

1 PETER 4:8

Above all, I love other people deeply because love covers over a multitude of sins. I also agree with You, God, about the proximity of my relationships! What You say is what I say, on earth as it is in heaven. Your will be done!

1 JOHN 3:18

I do not love with words or speech but with actions and in truth. I back my words with action! This is not just talk for me.

Chapter 19

SELF-CONFIDENCE

Like everyone, I have had ups, and I have had downs. But, I was raised to understand I was made in the image of God. I love being me! I'm the only me there will ever be! I think you can love yourself and not be prideful by realizing that God established your identity in the first place.

If you live a life submitted to God, you can find comfort in knowing that He wants you to become the person He has called you to be and to get into the places you're going to more than you desire to be there. I believe the key is complete submission to Him. We die to ourselves and lose our lives to find them. To "lose your life" means to lay down your way and self to take up the person God has created you to be. I am not saying we shut down our minds because I believe we are very much spirit, soul (mind, will, emotion), and body. However, I believe we can be the authentic, confident, and powerful person He has designed us to be—not just a replica of the world around us, but a reflection of Him.

The process of discovering the person we're called to be is a fun, adventurous journey of exploring. Knowing it's not about you anyway brings much comfort. It's all about the one who made you, created you, designed you, set you apart, and is placing you where you are going. Then your perspective changes. There isn't a false sense of shame or guilt or fear or regret. When it's all about Him, it's not all about you. Everything shifts to a different point of view.

When we obsess about ourselves, then insecurity runs rampant. But when God is the center, the beginning, the middle, and the end, everything starts and finishes with Him. It's easy when we remember we are made in His image. It's just not about you. *He is in need of you.*

The problem is that many people do love their neighbors as themselves, but they don't love themselves. God wants us to love ourselves. *He wouldn't have had you love your neighbor as yourself if you weren't going to love yourself.*

I don't think we serve God to serve our selfish ambitions. When we live a life surrendered to God, it is so completely fulfilling; it is a wild ride with Him and nothing but a heart submitted to the one who made us satisfies. The irony of that still is shrouded in mystery to me. I pray for people who seem to be lost in the maze of figuring out their meaning and purpose. I believe it's to be made in the image of God. It's to follow Him and do what we know to do daily and become more like Him, step by step, and love the people around us as we love ourselves.

SCRIPTURES USED IN THIS SECTION

"May your whole spirit, soul and body be kept blameless at the coming of our Lord Jesus Christ."
—1 THESSALONIANS 5:23B

"So God created mankind in his own image, in the image of God he created them; male and female he created them."

—GENESIS 1:27

FOR THE LOVE OF GOD

"The second is this: 'Love your neighbor as yourself.'
There is no commandment greater than these."
                                            —MARK 12:31

A PRAYER ON SELF-CONFIDENCE

If you want to know who you are, here's what you do

Read the Bible; it becomes like a mirror

You find out who you are supposed to be there

I know some parts are hard to understand

But that's part of that scavenger hunt, the adventure, man

We are crafted, sculpted, and made with so much love

There's more care for your hair than you could even think of

The Bible goes as far as to say, He knows the number of hairs on your head

Including the ones that you lose in your bed

If He cares about your hair, how much more does He care about you?

The things that matter to you matter to Him too

We're supposed to love our neighbor as much as we love ourselves

That means we are supposed to love ourselves just as much as anybody else!

You are made in His image, so let's be sure

That with a little heart adjustment you too can be pure

It doesn't take much, just a reminder who you are

Like Simba and his father, your real image isn't far

But oh, how easy it is to look away

To forget and start to stray

But go back in the Bible and fill yourself up

And love who you are—God sure does love this stuff

You are not the size of your clothes

Your bank statement or what you know

God has more thoughts about you than sand by the ocean

He's more concerned about your devotion

FOR THE LOVE OF GOD

So many people look to how many this or that
Or symbols of status that they don't have yet
But God is mindful of your deepest parts
He's way more aware of the condition of your heart
Your value and worth aren't in what you do
It's in what God thinks of you

SCRIPTURES USED IN THIS PRAYER

"Anyone who listens to the word but does not do what it says is like someone who looks at his face in a mirror and, after looking at himself, goes away and immediately forgets what he looks like. But whoever looks intently into the perfect law that gives freedom, and continues in it—not forgetting what they have heard, but doing it—they will be blessed in what they do." **—JAMES 1:23-25**

"It is the glory of God to conceal a matter; to search out a matter is the glory of kings." **—PROVERBS 25:2**

"I want them to be encouraged and knit together by strong ties of love. I want them to have complete confidence that they understand God's mysterious plan, which is Christ himself." **—COLOSSIANS 2:2, NLT**

"Indeed, the very hairs of your head are all numbered." **—LUKE 12:7A**

"The second is this: 'Love your neighbor as yourself.' There is no commandment greater than these." **—MARK 12:31**

"So God created mankind in his own image, in the image of God he created them; male and female he created them." **—GENESIS 1:27**

"Create in me a pure heart, O God, and renew a steadfast spirit within me." **—PSALM 51:10**

"We all, like sheep, have gone astray, each of us has turned to our own way; and the LORD has laid on him the iniquity of us all." **—ISAIAH 53:6**

"How precious are your thoughts about me, O God. They cannot be numbered! I can't even count them; they out-number the grains of sand! And when I wake up, you are still with me!" **—PSALM 139:17-18, NLT**

PERSONALIZED SCRIPTURE DECLARATIONS TO GIVE YOU AN IDENTITY REBOOT

JOSHUA 1:9

I am strong and courageous. I refuse to be afraid or discouraged because You, Lord my God, are with me wherever I go.

2 CHRONICLES 32:8

God, You are with me to help me fight my battles.

PSALM 20:7

Some trust in their earthly possessions and in their bank accounts, but I trust in Your name, my Lord and God.

PSALM 27:3

Though it may feel like an army has me surrounded, my heart will not fear; though war breaks out against me, even *then*, I will be confident.

PSALM 118:8

It is better to find a secure resting place in You, Lord, than to put our trust in people.

PSALM 139:13-14

You created the deepest place in me; You put me together in my mother's womb. I praise You because I am intentionally, respectfully, and wonderfully made. What You do is wonderful; I know that with all my heart.

PROVERBS 3:25-26

I do not fear sudden disaster or the ruin that overtakes

wicked people because You, God, will be at my side and will keep my foot from getting caught in a trap.

PROVERBS 3:32

Father, I know You hate things that are perverse, but You are friends with those who keep their hearts right!

PROVERBS 14:26

I respect You, God; therefore, I have a secure fortress in You, and for my children, it will be a refuge.

ISAIAH 26:3

You will keep me in perfect peace because my mind is fixed on You; I trust in You. So I keep my heart, my eyes, and my mind fixed on You!

ISAIAH 32:17

The fruit of Your righteousness in me will be peace, Jesus; its effect will be quietness and confidence forever.

ISAIAH 40:31

I place my hope in You, Lord, and that is when my strength is renewed. I soar on wings like eagles; I run and do not grow weary; I walk and do not faint. It's in You and through You that I do all things.

ISAIAH 41:10

No way am I fearful because, God, You are with me; I will not be discouraged because You are my God! You will strengthen me and help me; You will uphold me with Your righteous right hand.

JEREMIAH 17:7

I am blessed because I trust in You, Jesus; my confidence is in You.

1 CORINTHIANS 2:3-5

I came to You in weakness and with great fear and trembling. My message and my preaching were not with wise and persuasive words but with a demonstration of the Spirit's power so that others' faith might not rest on human wisdom but on God's power.

2 CORINTHIANS 3:2-4

I am a letter written on hearts, known and read by everyone, not written with ink but with the Spirit of the living God, not on tablets of stone but on tablets of human hearts. This confidence I have through Jesus before God.

2 CORINTHIANS 12:9

Your grace is enough for me; Your power is made perfect in my weakness! So, because of this, I boast all the more gladly about my weaknesses so that Jesus' power may rest on me!

EPHESIANS 3:12

In You and through faith in You, I may approach You, God, with freedom and confidence.

PHILIPPIANS 1:6

I am extremely confident that You who started a good work in me will carry it on to completion until the day of Jesus' coming back.

PHILIPPIANS 4:13

I can do all things through You, Jesus, who gives me strength! Show me what is in Your heart for me to do today!

2 TIMOTHY 1:7

Your Spirit, God, does not make me shy or shrink back, but exactly the opposite! It gives me power, love, and self-discipline.

HEBREWS 4:16

I approach Your throne of grace, God, with confidence so that I may receive mercy and find grace to help in my time of need.

HEBREWS 10:35-36

I do not throw away my confidence; it will be richly rewarded. I need to persevere so that when I have done Your will, God, I will receive what You have promised. I put my faith in You, God!

HEBREWS 13:6

I say with confidence, "Lord, You are my helper; I will not be afraid. What can people do to me?"

1 JOHN 5:14-15

This is the confidence I have in approaching You, God: that if I ask anything according to Your will, You hear me. If I know that You hear me—whatever I ask—I know I have what I have asked of You.

Chapter 20
TIME

Time is an extremely interesting measurement. You can't get more of it. Tomorrow turns into yesterday rapidly, and the weeks go by so fast. I love to pray over my days. We are only as good as our days are. We have very few days that are special-occasion-type days. We mostly have normal days, so I work to make those days great and fill them with significance by living a life worthy of the call and staying close to the heart of God. I do this by asking God, *What is on Your heart today?* And when I veer off, and my mind is wandering, or I can feel myself drifting into my own thing, I stop myself and check in with Him again. "Eyes up here" is a good guide. Are my eyes on Him?

I work to make the most of my time. I think of my days as presents, and I am deeply grateful for them and try to spend them wisely. I spend most of my life learning. I celebrate simple things. I invest in people. I labor to be efficient because our hours are precious.

I believe our highest and best use is spent obeying God, doing what He says, and living a life submitted to Him. He knows all things, and we can trust Him! Fearing God is the beginning of wisdom. Spending our time caring more about what God thinks than what other people think yields high dividends in the long run of our lives!

There really is a season for everything—A time for every-thing under heaven. When I rest, I work to rest well. When I play, I want to play hard. When I have fun, I want it to be good! When I dream, I want it to be sweet! Let's really be alive; this is our one life. Let's wake up; let's really live—acti-vated and resolute.

SCRIPTURES USED IN THIS SECTION

"Those who trust in themselves are fools, but those who walk in wisdom are kept safe."

—PROVERBS 28:26

"The fear of the LORD is the beginning of wisdom, and knowledge of the Holy One is understanding."

—PROVERBS 9:10

"There is a time for everything, and a season for every activity under the heavens."

—ECCLESIASTES 3:1

A PRAYER ON TIME

Time is a trip
It goes by so fast
The sand in the hourglass
It just doesn't last
So we have to be wise
With how we spend our time
Prioritize all the things
That You say are prime
Our days are so vital
They matter the most
Kind of makes you rethink
Our "stuff" and our "posts"
God, what do You
Want me to do today?
Show me! Make it clear
And I won't delay
Only to the right things
I want to be attracted
How can I spend my time right
And not get distracted?
I no longer look
To the left or the right
Heck no! I'm not about to
Live a lesser life!
Show me my blind spots
So I can improve
I want to change, God
My life is for You
Tick, tick, tock

I can hear the beat
There goes the clock
I want to move my feet
To be where You want me
Every step of the way
These 24 hours, Lord
I give You this day!

SCRIPTURES USED IN THIS PRAYER

"The life of mortals is like grass, they flourish like a flower of the field; the wind blows over it and it is gone, and its place remembers it no more." —**PSALM 103:15-16**

"Teach us to number our days, that we may gain a heart of wisdom." —**PSALM 90:12**

"Let your eyes look straight ahead; fix your gaze directly before you." —**PROVERBS 4:25**

"Search me, God, and know my heart; test me and know my anxious thoughts. See if there is any offensive way in me, and lead me in the way everlasting." —**PSALM 139:23-24**

"Direct my footsteps according to your word; let no sin rule over me." —**PSALM 119:133**

PERSONALIZED SCRIPTURE DECLARATIONS TO HELP YOU PUT YOUR TIME IN GOD'S HANDS

PSALM 31:14-15

I trust in You, Lord; I say, "You are my God." My time is in Your hands; rescue me from the hands of my enemies, from those who pursue me in the wrong way!

PSALM 55:16-17

As for me, I call to You, God, and You save me. When I am upset in the morning, at noon, or in the evening, I cry out to You, and You hear my voice.

PSALM 90:12

Teach me how precious life is so I can gain a heart full of wisdom.

PROVERBS 16:9

My heart may plan my course, but God, You establish my steps.

PROVERBS 21:5

Because I am diligent, my plans lead to success, just as laziness leads to poverty.

ECCLESIASTES 3:1-2

There is a time for everything and a season for every activity under heaven: a time to be born and a time to die, a time to plant, and a time to uproot.

T

TIME

ECCLESIASTES 3:11

God, You have made everything beautiful in its time. You have also set eternity in the human heart, yet no one can grasp what You have done from beginning to end.

ESTHER 4:14

I am right on time and not behind! I have been born for such a time as this.

EPHESIANS 5:15-17

I am very careful how I live—not as foolish but as wise, making the most of every opportunity because the days are evil. I am not centered on what I know; instead, I tap into Your wisdom, God, and I completely understand what Your will is.

2 PETER 3:8-9

But do not forget this one thing: with the Lord, a day is like a thousand years and a thousand years are like a day. God is not slow in keeping His promise, as some understand slowness. Instead, He is patient with us, not wanting anyone to dissolve into nothingness, but everyone to come to repentance by knowing God through Jesus.

1 JOHN 2:17

The world and its desires fade away, but whoever does the will of God lives forever.

Chapter 21

UNLEASH ON THE EARTH

God, I am asking You to visit us because we really need it. People are losing their cool. People who used to hold it together are now becoming unraveled at the seams. It's interesting the words they are speaking. Out of the abundance of their hearts, their mouths speak, and it's fascinating to hear the words pouring out of their hearts these days.

I know none of this is new to You, God. I know heaven is not in emergency mode. I know You have always been and always will be steadfast, but I ask for You to unleash Yourself on the earth! We need more of You!

You know I have had my moments, just like everyone else, when not the best things have come out of my heart, but that is just the thing: I've had to go back to the source and make things right so a pure stream can flow.

Basically, God, we all need You big time. I ask You to unleash Yourself on the earth because we all need more of You! People seem unhinged. Do a new thing. Will You not pour Your Spirit out, and please don't hold back because we need You more than ever!

SCRIPTURES USED IN THIS SECTION

"The good person out of the good treasure of his heart produces good, and the evil person out of his evil treasure produces evil, for out of the abundance of the heart his mouth speaks."

—LUKE 6:45, ESV

"What has been will be again, what has been done will be done again; there is nothing new under the sun."

—ECCLESIASTES 1:9

A PRAYER ABOUT UNLEASHING ON THE EARTH

God, Your eyes are searching for hearts that are committed to You

So You can strengthen us to do all You've called us to do

Here I am; I am willing. My life is in Your hands

I sit at Your feet and prepare for Your plans

Your ways are not our ways, and Your thoughts are not our thoughts

Unleash Your love on the earth; I cry out for the lost

The hurting and the broken, the desolate and confused

I know You hear every cry, including the abused

Open the floodgates of heaven and pour out Your blessing

We look to You to heal our land instead of all this stressing

What You can do in a minute exceeds what can be done by our natural hands

Thank You, God, for wisdom as we walk out Your plans

Your ways, Your timing, Your will, and Your strength

Your love can't be measured—there is no depth, height, or length

You make me feel secure; on You I place my feet

Your love is so unending; Your plans can't be beat

SCRIPTURES USED IN THIS PRAYER

"For the eyes of the LORD range throughout the earth to strengthen those whose hearts are fully committed to him." **—2 CHRONICLES 16:9A**

"Do not let me be put to shame, nor let my enemies triumph over me." **—PSALM 25:1**

"'For my thoughts are not your thoughts, neither are your ways my ways,' declares the LORD." —**ISAIAH 55:8**

"Oh, that you would rend the heavens and come down, that the mountains would tremble before you!" —**ISAIAH 64:1**

"'Bring the whole tithe into the storehouse, that there may be food in my house. Test me in this,' says the LORD Almighty, 'and see if I will not throw open the floodgates of heaven and pour out so much blessing that there will not be room enough to store it.'" —**MALACHI 3:10**

"If my people, who are called by my name, will humble themselves and pray and seek my face and turn from their wicked ways, then I will hear from heaven, and I will forgive their sin and will heal their land." —**2 CHRONICLES 7:14**

"But do not forget this one thing, dear friends: With the Lord a day is like a thousand years, and a thousand years are like a day." —**2 PETER 3:8**

"Teach me to do your will, for you are my God; may your good Spirit lead me on level ground." —**PSALM 143:10**

"So he said to me, 'This is the word of the LORD to Zerubba-bel: "Not by might nor by power, but by my Spirit," says the LORD Almighty.'" —**ZECHARIAH 4:6**

"He makes my feet like the feet of a deer; he causes me to stand on the heights." —**PSALM 18:33**

"I know that you can do all things; no purpose of yours can be thwarted." —**JOB 42:2**

PERSONALIZED SCRIPTURE DECLARATIONS TO CRY OUT FOR MORE OF GOD

NUMBERS 6:24-26

God, bless me and keep me; make Your face shine on me and be gracious to me. Will You turn Your face toward me and give me peace?

1 SAMUEL 16:7

People look at the outward appearance, but, Father, You look at the heart.

2 CHRONICLES 7:14

When Your people, who are called by Your name, humble ourselves, pray, seek Your face, and turn from our wicked ways, then You will hear from heaven, and You will forgive our sin, and will heal our land. So we humble ourselves, pray, seek Your face, turn from our wicked ways, and look to You! Forgive us and heal our land, God.

2 CHRONICLES 16:9

God, strengthen me because I am fully committed to You.

PSALM 23:1-4

Father, You are my shepherd; because of You, there is nothing that I need. You make me lie down in green pastures. You lead me next to quiet waters. You refresh my soul. Because of You, I can take a deep breath. You guide me along the right path, for Your name's sake. Even though I walk through the darkest valley, I will fear no evil; You are with me; Your rod and Your staff, they bring comfort to me.

PSALM 33:18-19

Because I respect and fear You, Lord, and want to please You the most, and I place my hope in Your unfailing love, You deliver me from death and keep me alive during hard times of utter chaos.

PSALM 36:7

I can't put a price on Your love because it never fails me! I take refuge in the shadow of Your wings.

PSALM 139:23-24

Search me, God, and know my heart; test me and know my deepest thoughts. See if there is any offensive way in me and lead me in the right way forever.

ISAIAH 44:3-4

God, pour water on my thirsty land and streams on the dry ground; pour out Your Spirit on my kids and Your blessing on my children and my children's children so that they will spring up like beautiful grass in a meadow, like full gorgeous trees by flowing streams. We need You now more than ever!

ISAIAH 58:11

Lord, You guide me always; You satisfy my needs and strengthen me. Because of You, I am like a well-watered garden, like a spring whose waters never fail.

JOEL 2:28

Father God, will You pour out Your Spirit on all people? So that our sons and daughters will prophesy, our old men will dream dreams, and our young men will see visions?

MICAH 7:18

God, You forgive my sin and my disobedience. You do not stay angry forever, but You take joy in showing me mercy. Thank You for Your new beginnings!

EZEKIEL 34:11

You said Yourself, God, that You will search for Your sheep and look after us.

2 CORINTHIANS 9:8

God, You are able to bless me to the point that it is more than enough so that in all things, at all times, in every issue, I have all that I need; I have more than enough for every good work!

U

UNLEASH ON THE EARTH

Chapter 22
VICTORY

I know the victory is God's. He is the one who actually has the ability to fight on my behalf when I allow it. So I look to Him to do that. Instead of defending myself in my own strength, I am walking the steps out with God and not just on my own.

There are several times when I have wanted to take up a battle myself, but I have learned that He wants to contend for me. It's so much better when we let Him fight on our behalf. So I allow God to be the one to battle on my behalf! When we do things in His strength, we get His strong results. So I focus on Him. I let Him into the battle. *Thank You, God, for the ability to walk with You. To go with You. You are so faithful to me, God.*

One of the things I labor for is to enter into His rest. Once I have given something over to Him, I work to keep it in His hand and do not take it back by worrying or taking matters into my own hands outside of Him. Fight for your peace. As we rest and trust Him to fight our battles for us, it is such a position of power. When we put our battles in His hands and take them out of our hands, it's amazing how He can do wonderful things for us.

That doesn't mean we do nothing. We certainly have a part to play in situations as He leads us! I believe in taking the steps we are supposed to when He asks us to. We co-labor with Him! But it's in Him, through Him, with Him where the victory lies.

When we give Him the position of authority in our lives to rule and reign, it's a unique, fantastic position of surrender. Let God be in charge and watch Him fight your battles. I'm talking absolute surrender. By real surrender, I mean, is God first? Let nothing and no one be before Him. Let God lead your life. When He is first and He truly leads you in it all, then you are walking in fear of God, who is greater than it all. We can never go wrong with pleasing God first.

When God vindicates you, it is on another level. It feels earth-shaking. So I want to encourage you to let Him fight on your behalf so you can enter into the next place. We are going to go to the other side. God is so good. He can be trusted.

SCRIPTURES USED IN THIS SECTION

"The horse is prepared for the day of battle, but the victory belongs to the LORD."
—PROVERBS 21:31, NLT

"The LORD will fight for you; you need only to be still."
—EXODUS 14:14

"Let us therefore be diligent to enter that rest, lest anyone fall according to the same example of disobedience."
—HEBREWS 4:11, NKJV

"That day when evening came, he said to his disciples, 'Let us go over to the other side.'"
—MARK 4:35

FOR THE LOVE OF GOD

"For the LORD is good and his love endures forever; his faithfulness continues through all generations."

—PSALM 100:5

V

VICTORY

A PRAYER ON VICTORY

I am fighting for the heart of my King

What matters to You matters to me

Today I won't tangle with civilian affairs

No more worry and toil, entertaining fears

I lift my eyes, and I look to You

It's amazing all the things that You've brought me through

My understanding of what's in the daily grind

That is what I think about most of the time

It's what determines my capacity

And how I can rise in what You've asked of me

Victory is Yours! That is what I say

I know the power is in Your secret place

I'm thankful for You, and I choose to remain

Right by Your side where You heal me from pain

There is a deep settling, a confident reassurance

That when I wait for You, I build up my endurance

SCRIPTURES USED IN THIS PRAYER

"No one serving as a soldier gets entangled in civilian affairs, but rather tries to please his commanding officer." **—2 TIMOTHY 2:4**

"I look up to the mountains—does my help come from there? My help comes from the LORD, who made heaven and earth!" **—PSALM 121:1-2, NLT**

"The LORD has done great things for us, and we are filled with joy." **—PSALM 126:3**

"The horse is made ready for the day of battle, but victory rests with the LORD." —**PROVERBS 21:31**

"He who dwells in the secret place of the Most High Shall abide under the shadow of the Almighty." —**PSALM 91:1, NKJV**

"And God raised us up with Christ and seated us with him in the heavenly realms in Christ Jesus." —**EPHESIANS 2:6**

"But those who hope in the LORD will renew their strength. They will soar on wings like eagles; they will run and not grow weary, they will walk and not be faint." —**ISAIAH 40:31**

PERSONALIZED SCRIPTURE DECLARATIONS TO HELP YOU GET THE VICTORY

DEUTERONOMY 20:4

Lord, my God, You are the one who goes with me to fight my battles on my behalf against the ones who attempt to raise a standard opposing me. You give me the victory!

2 SAMUEL 8:6B

God, You gave David victory wherever he went! I ask for that same victory in my own life!

PSALM 20:6

Now this I know: Father, You give the victory to Your anointed. You answer me from heaven with the victorious power of Your right hand.

PSALM 44:3

It was not by my sword that I won the land, or did the strength of my arm bring me victory; it was *Your* right hand, *Your* arm, and the light of *Your* face, because You loved me. To You be the glory, the honor, and all the praise for every victory that I win!

PSALM 44:6-7

I put no trust in my strength; my own thoughts or ideas do not bring me victory, but You give me victory over my enemies. You put my adversaries to shame.

PSALM 118:15

Shouts of joy and victory resound in the tents of the righteous. Lord, Your right hand has done mighty things!

PSALM 149:4

You, Lord, take delight in Your people; You crown the humble with victory.

PROVERBS 21:31

Victory rests with You, Lord.

ROMANS 8:37

I overcome everything through You because You love me.

1 CORINTHIANS 15:57

Thanks be to You, God! You give me the victory through Jesus.

Chapter 23
WORK, WORK, WORK

This is one of my favorite subjects. It's 5:24 a.m. and I'm typing by the fire and watching the sunrise. I love hard work! I also have had to fight to watch where I place my identity and to not falsely find my value in what I do when God says who I am is based on Him and in who He says I am.

I have gotten in the "working for my self-worth" trap before. Ha ha. Don't be judging. If you know about this rat race, then you can relate. If you don't, then it is easy to sit in the seat of the scoffer. But I'd love to throw you a rope and rescue you and say you don't have to achieve to become something great!

I am writing this book because I felt led to in my spirit by God, not because I wanted to! That is a huge difference from being an "accomplishaholic" like I used to be! I'd just start projects that were "good things." But I've heard it said that good is the enemy of great, and in God I believe that getting distracted into as many things as possible has been one of the biggest devices used against me in my life. I even got physically sick from it.

Now, I am learning to be led by God in all of my steps instead of sort of led and it is overhauling my way of thinking.

FOR THE LOVE OF GOD

The diligent hand will rule, but don't take it out of context like I used to. Be led by the Spirit of God. When your steps are ordered by Him, you are so much more effective.

SCRIPTURES USED IN THIS SECTION

"Blessed is the man who walks not in the counsel of the wicked, nor stands in the way of sinners, nor sits in the seat of scoffers."

—PSALM 1:1, ESV

"Diligent hands will rule, but laziness ends in forced labor."

—PROVERBS 12:24

"The steps of a good man are ordered by the LORD, And He delights in his way."

—PSALM 37:23, NKJV

W

WORK, WORK, WORK

A PRAYER ON WORK

I can't work to earn more love,
It wouldn't work anyway
I can't work to be of more value
You see past that every day
I can't work to be perceived
As a shinier toy
I can't do more "things"
To conjure up more joy
I know some people praise awards
But You know my every intention
Some others worship accomplishments
But accomplishments? You don't even mention
While people brag about sacrifice
Your eyes are looking for the deeper thing
It's not my works You're looking for but if I am obeying

SCRIPTURES USED IN THIS PRAYER

"For the word of God is alive and active. Sharper than any double-edged sword, it penetrates even to dividing soul and spirit, joints and marrow; it judges the thoughts and attitudes of the heart." —HEBREWS 4:12

"But by the grace of God I am what I am, and his grace to me was not without effect. No, I worked harder than all of them—yet not I, but the grace of God that was with me." —1 CORINTHIANS 15:10

PERSONALIZED SCRIPTURE DECLARATIONS INVITING GOD INTO YOUR WORK

PSALM 90:17

God, I ask for Your favor to be on my life and for You to establish what I work on.

PSALM 127:1

Unless You build the infrastructure of my household, God, I work in vain and just am essentially laboring in my own ability and not the Spirit. Unless You watch over the city, the guards stand and watch in their own strength for no reason. Let everything I do be in Your strength and not my own!

PSALM 139:14

I praise You, God, because I was made with care and wonder. Everything You do is worthy of praise; I know that with all my heart.

PROVERBS 16:3

I commit to You, Lord, whatever I do, and You establish my plans.

1 CORINTHIANS 15:58

I stand firm, and I refuse to let anything move me. I give myself with all of my heart to Your assignments, God, because I know that my efforts in You are not pointless! They are not without great gain! I do them by faith and unto You! No fear here! Establish Your plans in me!

W

WORK, WORK, WORK

2 CORINTHIANS 9:8

God, You have more than enough for me in every way to the point where I am overflowing so that in all things, at all times, having all that I need, I will prosper and in every single good work!

EPHESIANS 2:8-9

It is by grace I have received salvation, through faith— and this is not by what I have earned myself; it is Your gift, God— not by good behavior or good works, so that I can't brag about it.

EPHESIANS 2:10

I am Your masterpiece, God; I choose to stay focused on the things You ask me to do, which You prepared in advance.

COLOSSIANS 3:17

And whatever I do, if it's in what I say or in my actions, I do it all in Your name, Jesus. I give thanks to You, God my Father, through Your Son, Jesus.

COLOSSIANS 3:23-24

I put my whole heart into what I do, as if I am working for You, God, not for anybody else, since I know that I will receive an inheritance from You, Lord, as a reward. It is You, God, I am serving.

2 TIMOTHY 1:9-10

You have saved me and called me to a holy life, not because of anything I have done but because of Your purpose and grace! This grace was given to me in Jesus before the beginning of time, but it has now been revealed through the appearing of my Savior, Jesus, who has destroyed death and has brought life and immortality to light through Your message, Jesus.

2 TIMOTHY 2:15

I do my best to present myself to You, God, as someone You approve of, a worker who does not need to be ashamed and who correctly handles the word of truth.

TITUS 3:4-7

God, when Jesus became real to me, it was as if it was Your kindness and love showing up just for me, to save me! It was not because of the righteous things I did but because of Your mercy. You rescued me when I gave my heart to Jesus, and I am grateful for the Holy Spirit, whom You have poured out on me generously, without holding back, through Jesus, who delivered me from my sin. I am justified by Your grace so that I might have the hope of eternal life.

Chapter 24

X-RAY MY HEART

I am always willing to change. I want to keep advancing. I feel like that is the most exciting thing in life, even though it can also be extremely painful. We *choose our pain:* the pain of stagnation or the pain of growth. I will choose the pain of growth any day!

Raising the bar and going higher is so important, but I feel like some people just land and stay where they are and don't grow anymore after a certain point. I get it though; it is hard to face things. The interesting thing is that we don't know we are stuck in areas unless we have people who are willing to tell us the truth, to hold up a mirror to us and call us higher! So I love to be surrounded by people who challenge me!

I have learned to make it easy for people to tell me things. I try to thank people for telling me the truth. I also know most people hear something through the filter of their personalities and experiences. They forget to factor in who you are and consider where you are coming from and what you are saying, so I work to remain aware of this in my communication, and I always appreciate it when I am given the same respectful understanding. When someone does this, it is such a wonderful joy, and you get to be understood.

Being misunderstood has taught me the beauty of listening to people through the unfiltered lens of where *they* are coming from, not through what I would mean or where I have been. I try not to say, "I relate! I get it! I know how you feel." I sit in silence, share emotional space, and let them talk. I am reading the room. *Is this a moment I should speak or listen?* I ask myself. I try to remember not to correct or condemn and instead set myself to *listen*.

I have seen more power in letting someone be authentic and create a space and moment than I have in going in and giving my corrective dissertation on the subject matter. I have found my silence, and me being available emotionally is deeply necessary in the moment of trauma or drama, and not comparing stories or being on guard. It's time to be vulnerable and available and willing to grow.

A PRAYER TO FIND YOUR TRUE HEART

Show me my true heart, Lord, and how I can improve
I don't want to do anything that doesn't bring a smile to You
I know You've got that superhero X-ray vision
And I want to make changes; I don't want to cause division
So reveal to me right now how I can make things right
Show me anything I don't know; give me Your insight
I love You so much! You leave the 99 for the one
You never change, God, and You're so much fun
You're a creative King; You're holy and true
The closer I get, the more I want You
You're as faithful as the sun, as peaceful as the waves
I can trust You're always here, even on the mundane days
Show me *me* from Your perspective
Let me see Your point of view
There really isn't anything I want more than to please You

X

SCRIPTURES USED IN THIS PRAYER

"Search me, God, and know my heart; test me and know my anxious thoughts." —**PSALM 139:23**

"Do not be conformed to this world, but be transformed by the renewal of your mind, that by testing you may discern what is the will of God, what is good and acceptable and perfect." —**ROMANS 12:2, ESV**

"What do you think? If a man owns a hundred sheep, and one of them wanders away, will he not leave the ninety-nine on the hills and go to look for the one that wandered off?" —**MATTHEW 18:12**

X-RAY MY HEART

"I the LORD do not change." —**MALACHI 3:6A**

"And they were calling to one another: 'Holy, holy, holy is the LORD Almighty; the whole earth is full of his glory.'"—**ISAIAH 6:3**

"Jesus answered, 'I am the way and the truth and the life. No one comes to the Father except through me.'" —**JOHN 14:6**

"Come near to God and he will come near to you." —**JAMES 4:8A**

"Because of the Lord's great love we are not consumed, for his compassions never fail. They are new every morning; great is your faithfulness." —**LAMENTATIONS 3:22-23**

"Oh, that you had listened to my commands! Then you would have had peace flowing like a gentle river and righteousness rolling over you like waves in the sea." —**ISAIAH 48:18, NLT**

"For I always do what pleases him." —**JOHN 8:29B**

PERSONALIZED SCRIPTURE DECLARATIONS ASKING GOD TO SEARCH YOUR HEART

1 CHRONICLES 28:9

The wise King Solomon acknowledged You, God, and served You with wholehearted devotion and a willing mind. Lord, You search all of our hearts and understand every desire and each thought intimately. If I seek You, I will find You; but if I overlook You, You will reject me. God, how could I forget You? I want You to remain at the center of my priorities today!

2 CHRONICLES 16:9

Your eyes, Lord, go searching throughout the entire earth to strengthen the people whose hearts are entirely committed to You. I commit my heart to You!

1 SAMUEL 16:7

You, Lord, told Samuel, "Do not consider his appearance or his height, for I have rejected him. The LORD does not look at the things people look at. People look at the outward appearance, but the Lord looks at the heart." I am focusing on *my* heart. I want to keep my heart pure before You, Lord.

PSALM 4:4

I stand in reverence, and I do not sin; when I am on my bed, I search my heart, and I am silent.

PSALM 20:4

I am so grateful that You give me the desires of my heart and make all my plans succeed.

PSALM 26:2-3

Test me, Lord, and try me; examine my heart and my mind. I have always been mindful of Your unfailing love and have lived in reliance on Your faithfulness.

PSALM 34:18

You are close to the brokenhearted, and You save us when we are crushed in spirit and going through it!

PSALM 51:10

Create in me a pure heart, O God, and renew a steadfast and consistent spirit within me.

PSALM 139:23-24

Search me, God, and know my heart; test me and know my anxious thoughts. See if there is any offensive way in me, and lead me in Your way that is everlasting.

PROVERBS 3:5-6

I trust in You, God, with all my heart and refuse to get by on what I know; in everything I do, I submit to You, and You make my path straight.

PROVERBS 4:23

Above everything else, I guard my heart, because all of life flows from it.

PROVERBS 15:11

Death and destruction lie open before You, God—how much more does my heart open to You!

PROVERBS 21:2

A person may think their own ways are right, but You evaluate the intentions of the heart!

EZEKIEL 36:26

You give me a new heart and put a new spirit in me; thank You for removing from me a heart of stone and giving me a heart of flesh that is pliable and easy to work with!

MATTHEW 5:8

Blessed are the pure in heart, for we will see You, God.

ROMANS 8:27

And you who search my heart know the mind of the Spirit, because the Spirit intercedes for God's people in accordance with the will of God.

1 TIMOTHY 1:5

The goal of this command is love, which comes from a pure heart and a good conscience and a sincere faith.

HEBREWS 4:12

Your Word God is alive and active! It is sharper than any double-edged sword; it pierces even to dividing soul and spirit, joints and marrow. It differentiates the thoughts, motives, and attitudes of the heart.

1 PETER 3:3-4

My beauty and where I find my worth should not come from my outward appearance, as in my hair and jewelry or nice clothes. Instead, it should come from who I am

X

X-RAY MY HEART

inside, the unfading beauty of a gentle and quiet spirit, which is of great worth in Your sight, God. I know this doesn't mean I let myself go; I am after all Your temple since You live inside of me!

X

X-RAY MY HEART

Chapter 25

YESTERDAY, TODAY, AND FOREVER

Thank God, I can count on the fact that *He* never changes. That is a truth I can rely on. That is one thing I have never doubted. When there are plenty of questions I have had, that is one I have not. He indeed remains the same.

He loves everyone an equal amount, no matter what they have. No matter what their status is. No matter who they are related to. No matter what their job is. No matter where they live. Compassion flows from the heart of God. His loves flows. He forgives people, forgets our sins, and throws them into the sea of forgetfulness as far as the east is from the west. The drama of that captures my heart and reminds me how far God is willing to go to express that He has forgotten our sins!

I love how He loves our individuality. I love how He weeps with those who weep and He is right there in our grief. He gets in there with us and is present and bears down in whatever it is that we are dealing with. It's a mature kind of love. He's a weight-bearing-wall kind of love. It's a "firm foundation that I can bet my life on" kind of love.

I've learned to be honest and to talk to Him like a friend. But He's also a Father. You can go to Him with anything. He's a provider. He's the ultimate protector!

SCRIPTURES USED IN THIS SECTION

"I the LORD do not change."

—MALACHI 3:6A

"As far as the east is from the west, so far has he removed our transgressions from us."

—PSALM 103:12

"The LORD is close to the brokenhearted and saves those who are crushed in spirit."

—PSALM 34:18

Y

YESTERDAY, TODAY, AND FOREVER

A PRAYER TO THE UNCHANGING GOD

You never change; I mean never
When I look to You, I see forever
You're steady as the sun
As perfect as the rain
When I draw near to You
You ease my pain
I love You in the morning
And more by noon
But, God, I'm in awe by the time I see the moon
I am thankful for the ways You draw me by the river
When I lie still by You, You are quick to deliver
I am in Your ocean, in a geyser of Your love
I'm not leaving Your grace until I'm filled all the way up
When I'm anchored to You, I'm secure and sure
When I keep my eyes on You, I know I can endure
Even when I'm hurting, You stay right by my side
I run straight to You when things aren't going right
When I'm about to touch heaven and life is going great
You keep me steady because You remain the same

SCRIPTURES USED IN THIS PRAYER

"For I am the Lord, I do not change." —MALACHI 3:6A, NKJV

"Jesus Christ is the same yesterday and today and forever."
—HEBREWS 13:8

"The counsel of the LORD stands forever, the plans of his heart to all generations." —PSALM 33:11, ESV

"Be perfect, therefore, as your heavenly Father is perfect."
—MATTHEW 5:48

"But as for me, the nearness of God is my good; I have made the Lord GOD my refuge, That I may tell of all Your works." **—PSALM 73:28, NASB1995**

"Evening and morning and at noon I will pray, and cry aloud, and He shall hear my voice." **—PSALM 55:17, NKJV**

"How many are your works, LORD! In wisdom you made them all; the earth is full of your creatures." **—PSALM 104:24**

"He makes me lie down in green pastures, he leads me beside quiet waters." **—PSALM 23:2**

"Your love, LORD, reaches to the heavens, your faithfulness to the skies. Your righteousness is like the highest mountains, your justice like the great deep. You, LORD, preserve both people and animals." **—PSALM 36:5-6**

"We have this hope as an anchor for the soul, firm and secure." **—HEBREWS 6:19A**

PERSONALIZED SCRIPTURE DECLARATIONS ABOUT HOW WE CAN TRUST IN THE UNCHANGING GOD

NUMBERS 23:19

God, You are not human that You would lie; not a person that You would change Your mind. Do You speak and then not act? Do You promise and then not fulfill? No way! You do what You say, and I can trust You!

DEUTERONOMY 33:27

God, my eternal God, You are my refuge and I stay underneath Your everlasting arms. You get my enemies out of my way, demanding, "Destroy them!"

ISAIAH 40:8

The grass turns brown and the flowers fall and fade, but Your Word, God, withstands the test of time!

JOB 11:18

I am secure because there is hope; I look around me and take rest in Your safety.

PSALM 9:10

Those who know Your name trust in You, because You, God, have never left those who seek You.

PSALM 16:8

I keep my eyes always on You, God. With You at my right hand, there is no way I can be shaken.

PSALM 18:30

As for You, God, Your way is perfect. Lord, Your Word is flawless. You shield us all who take refuge in You.

PSALM 33:11

Your plans, Lord, stand firm forever, the purposes of Your heart through all generations.

PSALM 40:2

You lifted me out of the worst place of my life, out of the pit of despair; You stabilized my feet on a rock and gave me a firm foundation and place to stand so I will not sink!

PSALM 90:2

Before the mountains were born or You brought forth the whole world, from everlasting to everlasting *You are God*!

PSALM 102:25-27

In the beginning You laid the foundations of the earth, and the heavens are the work of Your hands. They will perish, but You remain; they will all wear out like a shirt. Like clothing You will change them, and they will be discarded. But You remain the same and Your years will never end.

PSALM 119:89

Your Word, Lord, is eternal; it stands firm in the heavens.

ISAIAH 40:28

Do people not know? Have they not heard? You, Lord, are the everlasting God, the Creator of the ends of the earth!

You will not grow tired or weary, and Your understanding no one can comprehend. I rest assured knowing this.

ISAIAH 41:10

I will not fear, because You, God, are with me; You strengthen me and help me; You uphold me with Your righteous right hand.

ISAIAH 54:17

No weapon formed against me will win, and You fight every tongue that fights against me. You take up my causes for me. This is my heritage because I am one of Your servants and this vindication is from You; You are the one who promised this, God.

DANIEL 7:14

You were given authority, glory, and sovereign power; all nations and people of every language worship You. Your dominion is an everlasting reign that will not pass away, and Your kingdom is one that will never be destroyed.

MALACHI 3:6

God, You do not change.

2 THESSALONIANS 3:3

Lord, You are faithful and keep me strong and protect me from the enemy.

2 TIMOTHY 2:13

Even when other people are faithless, God, You remain faithful.

HEBREWS 13:8

Jesus, You are the same yesterday and today and forever. I can rest assured thinking about that and relying on that promise.

JAMES 1:17

Every good and perfect gift is from You, God, coming down from the Father of the heavenly lights, who does not change like shifting shadows. I am so glad that I can count on the fact that You never change.

Y

YESTERDAY, TODAY, AND FOREVER

Chapter 26
ZZZZZZZZZZZ (SLEEP)

Well, sleep seems like it should be an easy one, but it hasn't been for me.

Some of my best times with God, and most inspired times creatively, have been while I'm up with the stars, so it's been sort of an odd thing for me to figure out. But I know that the Bible says He will give His beloved rest. It goes on to say that we are to labor to enter into rest. Okay, that one is wild for me and something I like to think about.

Laboring to enter into rest. For some people this isn't their struggle at all. Laziness is more their issue. Rest is important for our bodies, brains, creativity, quality of life (or so I hear, ha ha); this is something I'm working on daily. I don't have this one figured out—as I'm typing in the 4 a.m. hour—but I am excited to figure it out.

I have also learned that there are states of rest, as in peace of mind and learning to not worry. Some people deal with laziness and truly don't want to move out of their comfort zone. I have been fighting workaholic tendencies, which is the other extreme.

A good example is the story of Martha and Mary. If you don't know what that is, it is a famous story in the Bible about two sisters—one who sat at the feet of Jesus when He came to visit, and one who worked hard preparing every-thing for Him. So much so that one sister was annoyed and told on her to Jesus!

Martha said, "Jesus, look at her just sitting there while I do all the work!"

He said, "Yes, Mary chose the right thing. You too should be sitting at My feet spending time with me." *Jaw drop.*

The sin that so easily entangled Martha was that she was busy working—or what we would call "doing good works"—to get ready for Jesus, but she completely missed the good thing, which was sitting at His feet. Mary got it. Martha missed it so much that she went as far as to tell on Mary for not helping her to host Jesus. She wasn't even aware of it.

Real talk for a second. This is one of the sins that has so easily entangled me. It is one of the reasons I had hives in the first place: doing good things for Jesus but forgetting to sit at His feet. I was definitely not aware of the fact I was doing this.

What is the sin that so easily entangles you? I know we shouldn't be telling on each other; that is for sure. Ha ha. It just doesn't work out. Right now, there are these things fighting for our attention and our affection.

I guess there always have been distractions, but right now they are customized to play on our addictions. Our phones. Entertainment. Escaping reality. Being a workaholic. Being lazy. Whatever it is. God desires to be our first desire. *Sheesh.* This is a constant reset for every believer.

I know that learning isn't rest, so I have to stop listening to audio books, podcasts, and YouTube when I need to rest. Since we have access to unending amounts of education, entertainment, and games, we have to discipline ourselves to pace ourselves and wind down the way we are supposed to. We all have to eat, and most of us have a screen, but how we handle both of these things is crucial to the outcome of our sleep.

FOR THE LOVE OF GOD

Our health is closely related to our sleep. We are spiritual beings living in physical bodies and our needs need to be considered. I'm learning more and more about this subject every day. Bubble baths, lavender oil, turning off my electronics at the right time, even listening to peaceful sleep-inducing music—working to settle myself down is a work of art. I know this comes easy to some people, but some people have to put healthy sleep habits in place.

SCRIPTURES USED IN THIS SECTION

"In vain you rise early and stay up late, toiling for food to eat— for he grants sleep to those he loves."

—PSALM 127:2

"Let us, therefore, make every effort to enter that rest, so that no one will perish by following their example of disobedience."

—HEBREWS 4:11

"Therefore, since we are surrounded by such a great cloud of witnesses, let us throw off everything that hinders and the sin that so easily entangles. And let us run with perseverance the race marked out for us."

—HEBREWS 12:1

Z

ZZZZZZZZZZZ (SLEEP)

A PRAYER ON ZZZZZZZZZZZ (SLEEP)

Mind,

Stop wandering and be peaceful and still

I choose to believe that what God says is real

No matter the chaos or the raging seas

I can sleep in the boat with God working for me

Your Word is sure

Your Word is true

I'm confident You'll do what You said You would do

So, body, settle down!

As I take deep breaths

It's time to sleep; it's time to rest

I'm not needing to figure everything out

Now's not the time to know what it's all about

So I speak to the wind that's behind the waves

Calm down! God's in charge of all of my days

Z

SCRIPTURES USED IN THIS PRAYER

"He got up, rebuked the wind and said to the waves, 'Quiet! Be still!' Then the wind died down and it was completely calm." **—MARK 4:39**

"And we also thank God continually because, when you received the word of God, which you heard from us, you accepted it not as a human word, but as it actually is, the word of God, which is indeed at work in you who believe." **—1 THESSALONIANS 2:13**

"Suddenly a furious storm came up on the lake, so that the waves swept over the boat. But Jesus was sleeping." **—MATTHEW 8:24**

"Every word of God is flawless; he is a shield to those who take refuge in him." **—PROVERBS 30:5**

"For I am confident of this very thing, that He who began a good work in you will perfect it until the day of Christ Jesus." **—PHILIPPIANS 1:6, NASB1995**

"For he gives to his beloved sleep." **—PSALM 127:2B, ESV**

"The men were amazed and asked, 'What kind of man is this? Even the winds and the waves obey him!'" **—MATTHEW 8:27**

Z

ZZZZZZZZZZ (SLEEP)

PERSONALIZED SCRIPTURE DECLARATIONS TO HELP WITH SLEEP

PSALM 3:3-6

> But You, God, are a huge shield around me, my glory, the one who lifts my head high! I call out to You and You answer me. I lie down and sleep with peace in my heart; I wake again well rested in the morning because, God, *You did it again!* You have sustained me. No matter what the circumstances, I cast my cares on You and I know You are working all things out for my good. Even in the face of really hard issues with people, I cast them all over to You!

PSALM 4:8

> When I lie down, I go right to sleep because You alone, Lord, keep me safe. When I think about this, it calms me right down.

PSALM 121:7-8

> Lord, You keep me from all harm—You watch over my life and You watch over my comings and goings, both now and forever. I am so relieved by the access You have to my heart and life. Because You are watching over me, I can sleep with perfect peace.

PSALM 127:2

> I realize I can't be waking up early, staying up late, and expect to be well rested. I know I am not supposed to be filled with anxiety —*no!* I choose to be peaceful, because You give sleep to those You love.

PROVERBS 3:24

When I lie down, I refuse to be afraid; every time I go to rest, my sleep will be sweet!

JEREMIAH 31:26

Tomorrow I will wake up and report, "My sleep was pleasant to me."

MATTHEW 8:24

Jesus, when the storm suddenly and furiously came up on the lake and the waves swept over the boat, You kept sleeping! So, no matter what activity is swirling around me, I can be at peace knowing You are at work.

1 THESSALONIANS 5:10

Jesus, You died for me so that, even when I am awake or sleeping, I may live together in unity with You.

Be mindful about what you set your mind on. Where we place our affections is a big deal. It can be a subtle creep where you grow distant from God with the little things that cause your mind and heart to veer; that is coming directly from experience. Mind your heart. Watch it closely; from it flows all the issues of life! Those offenses that work to catch your gaze and run you in a completely different direction are not being thoughtful about your future. I have seen people's entire lives take a completely different course when they allowed very small, strategically placed hurts to turn into offenses. Watch it diligently. It can happen to anyone!

Stay humble and teachable. These two things are paramount for any advancement in God.

"Humble yourselves, therefore, under God's mighty hand, that he may lift you up in due time. Cast all your anxiety on him because he cares for you" (1 Peter 5:6-7).

There is always more of God. Even if you've been with Him for 40-plus years, there is still more. Keep yourself positioned under His waterfall; there is always something He has for you every single day! As you connect with Him and keep your spirit filled up with Him, it is so much easier to live a life where He is actually your God.

When we have an active and purposeful daily relationship with Him and He is in this daily fellowship with us, it's a beautiful thing. I have had both—seasons of not keeping myself fueled with Him, not utilizing the resources I have in His Word, filling myself up with distraction, comforting myself with other things, or attempting to because they all end up leading to a more upsetting outcome. But when I have set myself to seek Him, fill myself with the Word, worship Him consistently, tune out the things the world tries to entice me with, then my heart beats for Him. What we look at and focus on grows. *Look at Him. Gaze at Him. Focus on Him.* He is where it all begins and ends.

So find scriptures to support whatever you are dealing with and surround your world with those as a reminder. Put them on your wallpaper on your phone, in your car, bathroom, kitchen, by your bed. Repeat them, and speak them over your circumstances, yourself, and your loved ones, and watch your life change.

Without a vision God's people perish. Put your vision before you. I have done this with vision boards, books, calendar countdowns, goals on canvases and on the fridge and in my room and on my phone and in my car. Surround your life with where you are going, not with where you are. As a man thinks in his heart, so is he!

Pray and talk to God! You are always on His mind. There is nothing too difficult for Him or too small or too big for Him. Bring your circumstances to Him; He already knows about it anyway!

Get filled with the Holy Spirit. When Jesus died on the cross, He said He had to go on so the greater one could come, which was the Holy Spirit. The Holy Spirit is the comforter, the guide, our friend; He is so helpful. If He is not in operation in your life, I recommend you ask Him to come into your world and do what only He can do. Ask if you can be filled with the Holy Spirit with the evidence of speaking in tongues! You can right now from wherever you are! In the book of Acts, it says everyone in the upper room was filled and spoke in tongues. Some people believe those gifts are not for today, but I don't want you to miss out on this because it is so wonderful. I do not know where I would be without it. It is so great to live a Spirit-led life; it has brought me freedom.

Also, find a church. That will be a game-changer. It will be amazing to have a church to be a base, a family, and a stabilizer for you. Remember, they are full of people and are not perfect. Allow God to lead you and do not be easily offended in the process but know how good God is and how much church is His idea!

Thank you for reading this book! Please share it with people as you feel led to and let me know the impact it has had on you. That would mean so much to me!

Love you!

Chelsea Perry

SCRIPTURES USED IN THIS SECTION

"Be strong and courageous. Do not be afraid or terrified because of them, for the LORD your God goes with you; he will never leave you nor forsake you."
—DEUTERONOMY 31:6

"Jesus Christ is the same yesterday and today and forever."
—HEBREWS 13:8

"Above all else, guard your heart, for everything you do flows from it."
—PROVERBS 4:23

"Therefore, since we are surrounded by such a great cloud of witnesses, let us throw off everything that hinders and the sin that so easily entangles. And let us run with perseverance the race marked out for us, fixing our eyes on Jesus, the pioneer and perfecter of faith. For the joy set before him he endured the cross, scorning its shame, and sat down at the right hand of the throne of God."
—HEBREWS 12:1-2

"For from him and through him and for him are all things. To him be the glory forever! Amen."

—ROMANS 11:36

"He said to me: 'It is done. 'I am the Alpha and the Omega, the Beginning and the End.'"

—REVELATION 21:6A

"For as he thinks in his heart, so is he."

—PROVERBS 23:7A

"When the day of Pentecost came, they were all together in one place. Suddenly a sound like the blowing of a violent wind came from heaven and filled the whole house where they were sitting. They saw what seemed to be tongues of fire that separated and came to rest on each of them. All of them were filled with the Holy Spirit and began to speak in other tongues as the Spirit enabled them."

—ACTS 2:1-4

THANK YOU

Thank you to everyone who helped edit and pray and for all the contributors through the process of this book! I am thankful for you!

ABOUT THE AUTHOR

Chelsea Perry is an in-demand speaker, songwriter, author, and entrepreneur. Having written over 500 songs and 19 musicals for kids, she is passionate about the power that music brings in positively changing lives.

Chelsea has been a pastor for over 20 years and has a deep desire to help people discover their purpose in life.

In her free time, Chelsea enjoys writing, going on adventures, and expressing her life through art.

Lightning Source UK Ltd.
Milton Keynes UK
UKHW010119180223
417112UK00001B/83